TEXT STRUCTURES
AND FABLES

GRADES 3–12

To my parents, who embody fairness, humility, and wisdom

—Gretchen

To my grandma, who embodied generosity, acceptance, and strength

—Jayne

TEXT STRUCTURES AND FABLES

GRADES 3–12

Teaching Students to Write About What They Read

Gretchen Bernabei
Jayne Hover

CORWIN Literacy

FOR INFORMATION:

Corwin

A SAGE Company

2455 Teller Road

Thousand Oaks, California 91320

(800) 233-9936

www.corwin.com

SAGE Publications Ltd.

1 Oliver's Yard

55 City Road

London EC1Y 1SP

United Kingdom

SAGE Publications India Pvt. Ltd.

B 1/I 1 Mohan Cooperative Industrial Area

Mathura Road, New Delhi 110 044

India

SAGE Publications Asia-Pacific Pte. Ltd.

18 Cross Street #10-10/11/12

China Square Central

Singapore 048423

President: Mike Soules

Vice President and Editorial Director: Monica Eckman

Director and Publisher, Corwin Classroom: Lisa Luedeke

Senior Content Development Manager: Julie Nemer

Associate Content Development Editor: Sarah Ross

Editorial Assistant: Nancy Chung

Project Editor: Amy Schroller

Copy Editor: Erin Livingston

Typesetter: C&M Digitals (P) Ltd.

Proofreader: Lawrence W. Baker

Cover Designer: Gail Buschman

Marketing Manager: Megan Naidl

Printed in the United States of America

Library of Congress Cataloging-in-Publication Data

Names: Bernabei, Gretchen S., author. | Hover, Jayne, author.

Title: Text structures and fables : teaching students to write about what they read, grades 3-12 / Gretchen Bernabei, Jayne Hover.

Description: Thousand Oaks, California : Corwin Literacy, [2023] | Includes bibliographical references.

Identifiers: LCCN 2022033330 | ISBN 9781071894248 (paperback) | ISBN 9781071901458 (epub) | ISBN 9781071901472 (epub) | ISBN 9781071901489 (pdf)

Subjects: LCSH: Composition (Language arts)—Study and teaching (Elementary)—Activity programs. | Composition (Language arts)—Study and teaching (Secondary)—Activity programs. | English language—Composition and exercises—Study and teaching (Elementary) | English language—Composition and exercises—Study and teaching (Secondary) | Fables—Study and teaching (Elementary) | Fables—Study and teaching (Secondary) | Educational tests and measurements—Texas.

Classification: LCC LB1576 .B4836 2023 | DDC 372.62/3044—dc23/eng/20220803

LC record available at https://lccn.loc.gov/2022033330

This book is printed on acid-free paper.

22 23 24 25 26 10 9 8 7 6 5 4 3 2 1

Contents

Visit the companion website at
resources.corwin.com/textstructuresandfables
for downloadable text structures, fables, and other
resources related to *Text Structures and Fables*.

Acknowledgments

We deeply appreciate our Corwin Literacy family: Lisa Luedeke, Tori Bachman, Julie Nemer, Sarah Ross, Sharon Wu, Nancy Chung, Gail Buschman, Melanie Birdsall, and Amy Schroller.

We love growing and learning together with our extended Trail of Breadcrumbs family: Dave and Judi Reimer, Nicole Morales, Honor Moorman, Stephen and Kayla Briseño, Stacy Lewis, Maureen Uclés, Amy Doege, Dottie Hall, Jennifer Martin, Alicia Narvaez, Gina Graham, Marie Cleary, Paul Erickson, Jennifer Payne, and Catherine McGough.

Tireless literacy leaders: Elizabeth Stephens, Nanette Roska, Carol Booth Olson, Jowie Walker, Stacy Horton, Beth Moore, Barbara Wells, Jennifer Robertson, Jeannie Istre, Gregory Reeves, Jim Lorenz, Brandian Bufford, Rene Jackson, Caron Sharp, Susan Diaz, Christine Evans, Prissy Peters, Amber Renteria, Gil-Rey Madrid, Adrienne Horton, Jana Andrews, Lydia Walden, Cori Spellane, Zulma Vasquez, Veronica Cuenca-Wilson, Betsy Asheim, Michelle Garza, Marsha Santos, Cesar Lopez, Melissa Skinner, Beth McDaniel, Mantequilla Green, Beth Klammer, Melanie Mayer, Jennifer Martin, Lorrie Payne, Roxane Greer, Stephanie Cash, Ashley Grahmann, Miguel Guhlin, Becky Waller, Katherine Pearce, Dana Felts, Kristi Mullins, Ashley Evans, Jennifer Sisk, Kila Bach, Shona Rose, and Tim Martindell.

Dedicated teachers: Michelle Hopkins, Susan B. Garcia, Dana Cullimore, Vanessa Griffith, Crystal Modawell, Stacy Sauerwein, Amber Owens, Mary Coleman, Paige Castellon, Dina Hinojosa, Melinda Bonkosky, Sharon McGrew, Melody Kneupper, LaShanda Moss-Hill, Lisa Reeves, Edith O'Canas, Craig Price, Arian Garza, Bonnie Cabeza, Natalie Gonzalez, Lisa Taiclet, Feliciano Garcia, Cheryl Baca, Melissa Thompson, and Ken Light.

Kubasaki Dragons: Kathleen Volkmann, Rona Tison, Dave Tarbell, Vanessa Van Dyken, Kathleen Nygard, Jill Bradshaw, Linda Centell, Richard Lee, Allen Trivett, Mary Sullivan-Trivett, Linda Westerberg, Tim Gilliland, Carol Canavan, Mark Wellman, Ami Warren, and Lisa Van Dyken.

Finally, especially from Gretchen: Mary Sue, Matilde and Julian, Bert and Dixie.

And from Jayne: Thank you, Jim, for being a supportive, encouraging, helpful husband. Your generous spirit gives me all I need to pursue my dreams.

Introduction

Tell me are we in danger?
If we like to fight
Like children
You're wrong, I'm right.

—Matilde Bernabei (2020)

Looking around our communities, it's hard to miss the cultural and political polarization that is creating lines in the sand and turning opponents into enemies. Many of my friends and family express sadness that we have forgotten how to hear each other.

We believe that hearing is not really the weakness. The problem lies with the invisibility of the mental reactions of a listener or reader. We suspect that most students (and many adults) have no idea of the power of their words; often, they are completely floored to hear that someone else absorbed their words with pleasure, with pain, or with any additional thought.

In Texas, the curriculum standards (known as the TEKS) were rewritten and approved in 2017 to go into effect in 2020. One of the most important yet formerly neglected major strands in this new set of standards is Strand 1, which prominently features "listening and speaking." The art of listening mirrors the art of reading. Real listening is not a passive activity, and neither is real reading. Furthermore, real listening is not the same as compliant silence. But so many teachers express frustration when trying to figure out how to incorporate listening into a room full of boisterous youngsters whose listening skills are hardly fully formed.

The aim of this book is to help students learn to consider their listener and to articulate their mental reactions to what they hear or read.

Its other aim is to equip teachers with manageable activities to help develop students' abilities to share aloud and in writing those thoughts that are their own as well as responses to whatever they may have heard or read and to hear—really hear—the thoughts of others. There has rarely been a more urgent need than now.

About Fables

On every school campus in this world, educators know their moral imperative: to develop students' literacy and citizenship skills. One of the world's earliest genres presents right and wrong with short and elegant simplicity: fables.

Nonetheless, I've stayed away from fables as teaching tools until now, probably because of their sledgehammer preaching. "If you lie, people won't believe you when you tell the truth." Yeah, yeah, got that. Mark Twain would argue that if people knew you had lied, you didn't do it well. The industrious ant survived while the musical grasshopper played all summer. So, music is never as valuable as food production? There go the arts. Slow and steady wins the race? Hardly ever, when other humans are involved. I have so often passed up the blunt force of that sledgehammer moral, choosing something besides fables as a classroom tool for character development.

But this year, I gave fables another look. Those three were the only fables I remembered clearly, but Jayne Hover brought me 147 others. We read through them, marveling at their charm, chuckling at the characters, discussing the morals, and seeing often-contradictory thoughts from multiple points of view. Isn't this what we want our students to do? To be more thorough, more exploratory thinkers than just "you're wrong—I'm right"?

What one side defines as a "moral value" may not be what the other side believes. In fact, maybe there are more than two sides. Perhaps our real senses lie in the vast area of the ambiguous, of the conditional, of the situational. So, to help our students navigate, we need better tools than a sledgehammer. And if they can chuckle and marvel as they read, they will have more to say. Fables are the perfect texts for this.

In addition to the treasury of fables, you can use the lessons to guide your students through five different concrete ways to write responses to readings (in this case, the fables). These include the following:

1. Writing basic responses to the reading
2. Writing fiction inspired by the text
3. Writing essays about the moral
4. Answering open-ended questions about the text
5. Using nontraditional formats to show you read it

Some teacher guides say, "Have students develop this thought"—leaving the teacher wondering *how*. The pages here will actually show you how to lead students through the thought processes, one step at a time.

How Do I Use This Book?

What's Your Instructional Wish?

I wish students would interact with a text on their own. (Use Part I.)

I wish students knew what it was like to be the author. (Use Part I.)

I'd like to give them more practice at answering questions about a text. (Use Part II.)

I'd like to give them some non-test prep for showing more deep understanding of a text. (Use Part III.)

How Else Can I Use This Book?

You can use the response lessons with any texts in any genre. You can also give students a list similar to the one below and allow them to choose how to respond.

Use text evidence from a fable to answer any of the following:

Why is honesty important to you personally?

Who's more helpful, the lion or the mouse?

Compare/contrast how greed is shown in two different fables.

Write a sequel to this fable.

Do you agree with this moral? What current event can illustrate your thoughts?

How does the author show that the fox is wise?

There are so many fables. Whatever theme you are working with, there are plenty of fables to pair. And when you give students a solid, strong pathway to learn how to respond, they will gradually answer any of the above questions with clarity and precision.

Students can practice with fables and then apply the processes to poems, excerpts from stories, nonfiction articles, speeches—anything. What could be more satisfying than using literature to help students articulate their developing citizenship?

What Do These Lessons Look Like in My Classroom?

Most of our work begins in our classroom journals. If you thumbed through a student journal in my classroom, you would see pages as varied as those shown here.

A self-generated routine journal entry (no prompt, no topic)

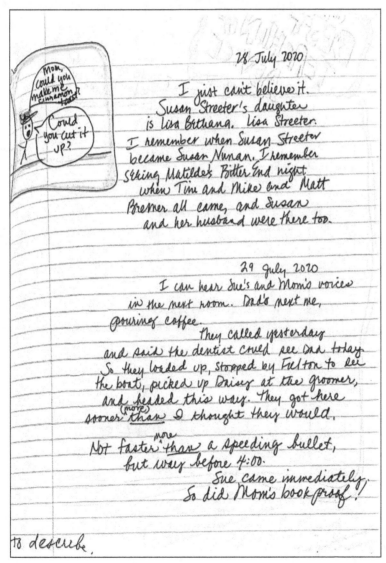

Notes on a craft lesson for "ba-da-bing" sentences, with a before and after sentence

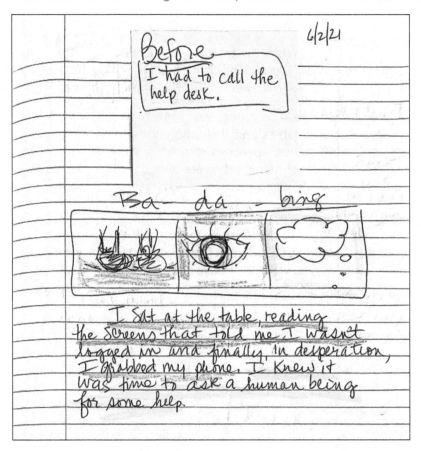

A three-things response to "The Ant and the Grasshopper"

Create or choose a question.

- Write some questions to show understanding of the characters, plot, themes, or vocabulary used in the fable

These questions stems range from basic to more complex understanding.

1. What happens in this fable? (Retell the story.)
2. What is this fable mostly about?
3. How do you think _____ feels at the beginning and/or end?
4. What is the conflict or problem in the fable? (How is it solved?)
5. Who is more _____ (helpful, nicer), _____ or _____?
6. How does _____ change during this story?
7. Why does _____ do/think/say/believe/want _____?
8. What's one word you would use to describe the _____ (character)?
9. What lesson does _____ learn in the fable?
10. What does the moral mean?
11. In sentence _____, what does the word or phrase _____ suggest?
12. How are _____ and _____ alike/different?
13. Why does _____ become _____ (upset, happy...) when _____?
14. What does _____ (character) mean when he says _____?
15. What can the reader tell (conclude) from the action in sentence(s) _____?
16. What does _____'s reaction when he learns _____ show about his character?
17. How do the actions of _____ and/or _____ support the theme/moral?
18. Write a summary using 3 details from the fable.
19. What causes _____ to realize _____?
20. Which sentence expresses a turning point in the fable?
21. Why does _____ agree to _____?
22. What is _____'s attitude about _____?
23. What argument does ___ (character) make to support his behavior/position/opinion?
24. What challenge(s) does _____ face?
25. What does _____ represent in the fable?
26. On which persuasive technique does _____(character) rely?

Explaining a Change

| how ___ changes in the story | at the beginning (with evidence) | at the end (with evidence) | another way to describe the change |

#9. What lesson does the Goat learn in the Fable?

7. Why does the goat believe the wolf is only thinking of his own appetite?
— Mrs. Peyton

19. What causes the goat to realize he should not come

...hat is the goat's attitude about the wolf's offer?
— Shuny Simper

The Wolf and the Goat

A hungry Wolf spied a Goat browsing at the top of a steep cliff where he could not possibly get at her. "That is a very dangerous place for you," he called out, pretending to be very anxious about the Goat's safety. "What if you should fall! Please listen to me and come down! Here you can you want of the finest, tenderest grass in the country." The Goat looked over the edge of th "How very, very anxious you are about me," she said, "and how generous you are with your gr I know you! It's your own appetite you are thinking of, not mine!"

Moral: An invitation prompted by selfishness is not to be accepted.

23. what argument does the wolf make to support his position.
Kat

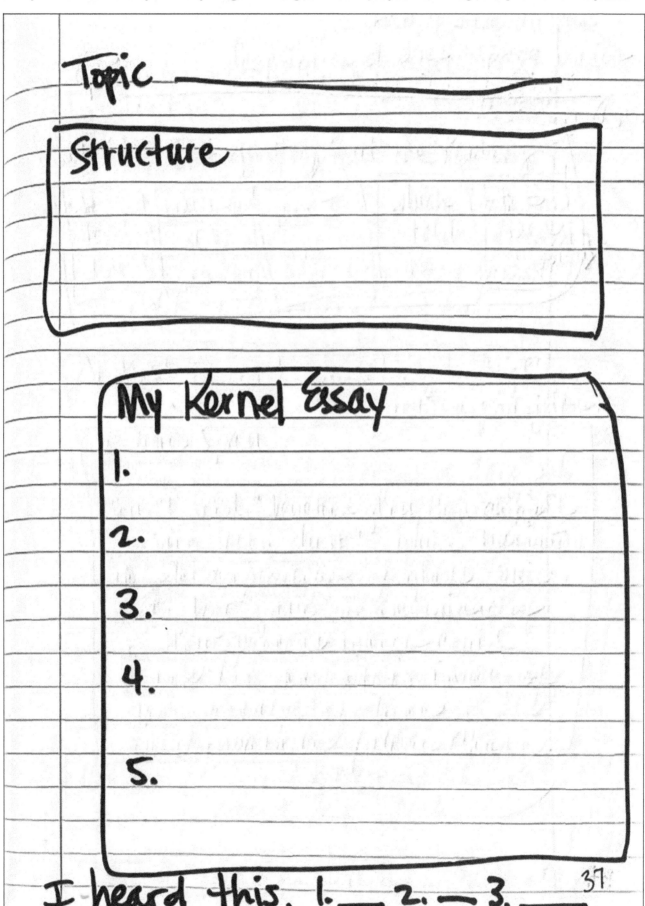

Topic _____

Structure

My Kernel Essay

1.

2.

3.

4.

5.

I heard this. 1. ___ 2. ___ 3. ___   37

Exploring the Relationship Between the Writer and the Reader

Readers and writers are speakers and listeners. It's the same relationship with the same back-and-forth volley of conversation. If it's a spoken conversation, we hear both sides; but if the words are written down, the conversational volley is visible only to one side. The reader may be reacting but those reactions would mostly be invisible to a bystander.

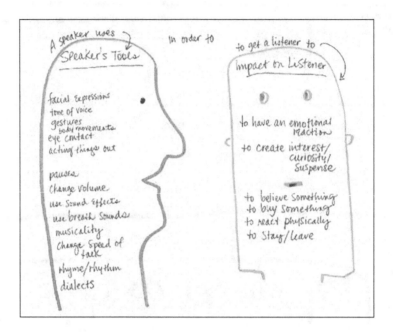

But the reactions are the most important focus of the lessons in this book. Every step of any of the lessons here places the student squarely into one or the other of these two heads. If they are learning craft, writing kernel essays, or reading essays to a partner, they perform the role of the writer, using the writer's tools or craft in order to have an effect on the reader.

If they are reading something, they notice some effect the text is having on them. They are in the role of the reader. Then, when they write a response, they switch roles again and use the writer's tools to react to what they have read.

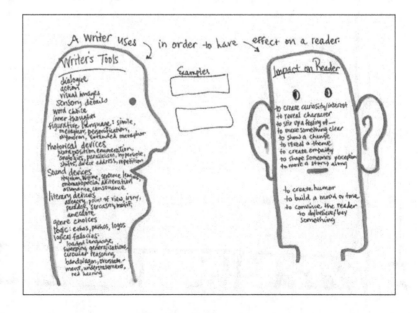

The two heads give you an outside view that helps you see what happens between the reader and the writer, and that impact continues to have a life when we react to what we read. Here's an example: Recently, a group of teachers read a poem by Sheila Black called "Possums" (2017). Afterward, they wrote their own poems using a similar thought and structure.

C. E. Price, one of the teachers in the group, wrote the poem "Stir Crazy." After his peers read his poem, they used the question stems to create one question each.

Stir Crazy

I have a buddy who over stirs.

Twirl, twirl, twirl

Clinkety, clinkety, clink

Stirring and stirring as his coffee is whirling –

The spoon might grind a hole in his mug I think!

Nerves you may ask? I have to deny –

for I have seen this man perform under fire –

cool as an arctic breeze – no shaking of his knees.

So no, not nerves – just a compulsion to stir,

His spoon will probably continue to whirl – long after his exit from this world.

C. E. Price

---

8. What is one word you would use to describe the speaker? Jessica Carlos

...speaker or the buddy? – Mariallan

"the spoon will probably continue to whirl" suggest... Estella

...at the beginning or End of the poem? Estella

20. What sentence expresses a turning point in the point. Nelda

6. How does the author's attitude toward the buddy change in the poem? John Clark

narrator's speakers attitude about stirring? Belinda

11. In line 8, what does the simile suggest? – Lisa Castellano

1. Why does the buddy have a compulsion to stir? – Laura

24. What challenge does the author of the poem face? – Dina

Questions for "Stir Crazy"

11. In line 8, what does the simile suggest?

Create or choose a question.

- Write some questions to show understanding of the characters, plot, themes, or vocabulary used in the fable.

These questions stems range from basic to more complex understanding.

1. What happens in this fable? (Retell the story.)
2. What is this fable mostly about?
3. How do you think _____ feels at the beginning and/or end?
4. What is the conflict or problem in the fable? (How is it solved?)
5. Who is more _____ (helpful, nicer), _____ or _____?
6. How does _____ change during this story?
7. Why does _____ do/think/say/believe/want _____?
8. What's one word you would use to describe the _____ (character)?
9. What lesson does _____ learn in the fable?
10. What does the moral mean?
11. In sentence _____, what does the word or phrase _____ suggest?
12. How are _____ and _____ alike/different?
13. Why does _____ become _____ (upset, happy...) when _____?
14. What does _____ (character) mean when he says _____?
15. What can the reader tell (conclude) from the action in sentence(s) _____?
16. What does _____'s reaction when he learns _____ show about his character?
17. How do the actions of _____ and/or _____ support the theme/moral?
18. Write a summary using 3 details from the fable.
19. What causes _____ to realize _____?
20. Which sentence expresses a turning point in the fable?
21. Why does _____ agree to _____?
22. What is _____'s attitude about _____?
23. What argument does ___ (character) make to support his behavior/position/opinion?
24. What challenge(s) does _____ face?
25. What does _____ represent in the fable?
26. On which persuasive technique does _____ (character) rely?

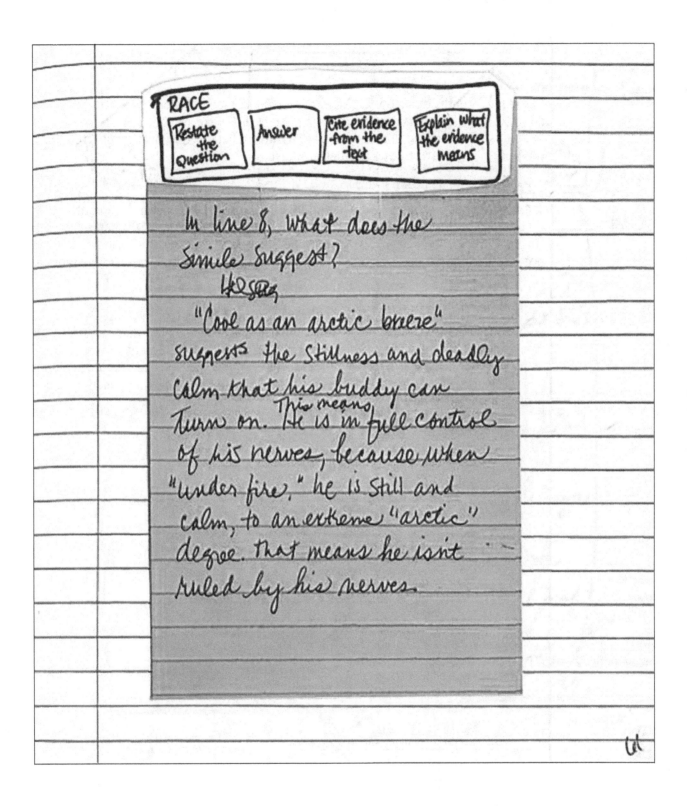

RACE

Restate the Question | Answer | Cite evidence from the text | Explain what the evidence means

In line 8, what does the simile suggest?

"Cool as an arctic breeze" suggests the stillness and deadly calm that his buddy can turn on. *This means,* He is in full control of his nerves, because when "under fire," he is still and calm, to an extreme "arctic" degree. That means he isn't ruled by his nerves.

Then each person chose a question and a structure. They wrote and shared their answers. As the poet listened, he experienced firsthand the impact of so many of his choices.

We hope the lessons in this book help you and your students make new discoveries about the impact of what we read as well as what we write.

The Book's Three Sections

Part I: Building Strong Readers and Writers

In the first months of school, these foundational routine practices build the skills that students will need when it's time for assessment. These lessons give ownership to the students, providing practice for students to articulate their own thoughts without prompts or questions from a teacher or a test.

Part II: Assessing Strong Readers and Writers

In order to shape students' facility at crafting a high-quality answer to a constructed response question (whether short or extended), we give students practice in both writing the questions as well as writing the answers. As always, the students choose not only their content but also the structure that brings out their best understanding of what they've read.

Part III: Using Nontraditional Formats

Frequently, teachers need to see visible evidence that students have grasped a concept or completed some reading. This evidence can take many different forms, and we share here our favorite five formats for students to show they did their reading without a single worksheet. Though ELAR teachers love to use these, they are also especially useful among content-area teachers.

Part I

Building Strong Readers and Writers

There's no substitute for direct, explicit, clear instruction.

Before we ask students to answer questions on a test—before we ask them to analyze on demand the effect of an author's choices on their audience of readers—our students must have some of those experiences as readers. **They must be the reader being affected**. They must be the person who said, "Ah! This character is a scoundrel!" or "This part brought a lump to my throat."

Our students need to wear the hat of the reader and the writer as often as we can build it into our days. They might wear the hat of the writer for a few short minutes as the class looks at one of their sentences to admire its power or for longer when they share their writing.

The three lessons in this part help build a routine for using language to respond to reading. Moreover, these three lessons all put a person in contact with another person. They build relationships. And isn't that what reading and writing are really for?

On the '90s TV series **Northern Exposure**, the poet/DJ Chris Stevens said, "If music is the pathway to the soul as Voltaire suggested, then speech is the pathway to other people. Live in silence and you live alone" (Smolan, 1991).

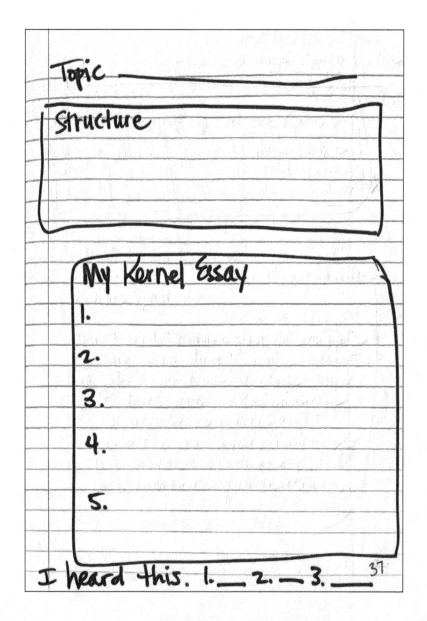

LESSON 1. RESPONDING TO READING

Your students have read a story; then the discussion goes something like this:

> You: What did you think about that story?
>
> A third of them: It was okay.
>
> Another third: It was boring.
>
> Another third: It was good.

With too little guidance, students don't have much to say, while too much guidance looks like test prep worksheets with correct answers built in. And do they need practice test questions for every single thing they read?

In fact, they don't need a question at all in order to make a comment, but they do need to know what they're being asked to do. This lesson gets them into the habit of generating a text-based, in-depth response from their swirling brainwork.

Text Structures for Basic Reader Response

Story of my Thinking

I used to think	But this happened	So now I know

Character Feelings

_____ felt _____	I know because they _____	I also know because they said _____

Making a Connection

When I read _____	I made a connection to (self, text, world)	Because _____ _____

Summary

Somebody wanted _____	But _____	So _____	Then _____

The Effect of an Author's Choice

The author uses... (choose one) ☐ Vocabulary ☐ Sensory Images ☐ Figurative language ☐ Something else (name it) _____	An example	Another example	This creates... (choose one) ☐ A _____ mood ☐ A _____ feeling ☐ An understating of _____ ☐ Something else _____

Step 1. Read a fable.

- Read or listen to a fable.
  - You could read more than one fable grouped in the same theme.
  - You could read or listen to a partner read a fable.
- These fables are short; reread the fable again and again to pick up hidden details.
- You may want to consider acting out the fable to internalize the story.

Step 2. Choose and use a text structure.

- Choose a text structure from the basic response structures.
- Let the structure help you write down what you noticed as you were reading.
- When you have written something to go with each box, you have written a kernel essay.

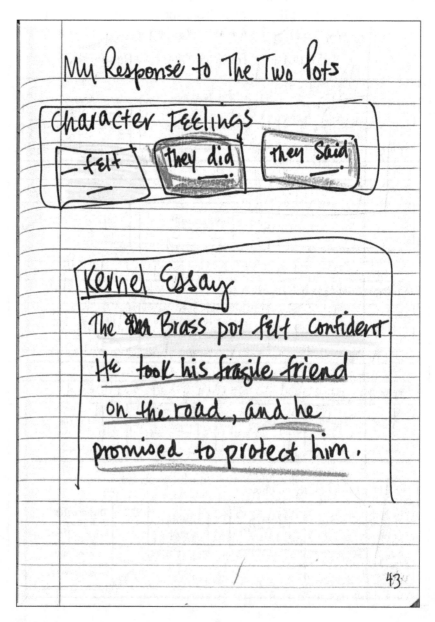

Step 3. Share.

- Read your kernel essay aloud to a partner or group.
- Listen to a couple of kernel essays written by others.

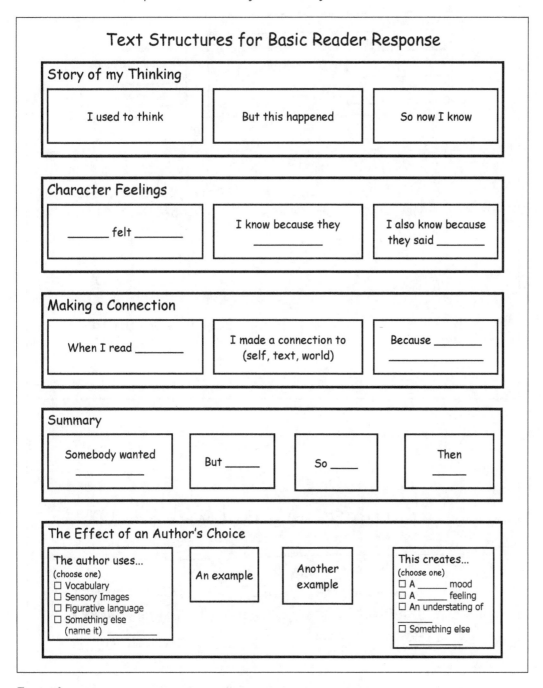

Text Structures for Basic Reader Response

Story of my Thinking

| I used to think | But this happened | So now I know |

Character Feelings

| _____ felt _____ | I know because they _____ | I also know because they said _____ |

Making a Connection

| When I read _____ | I made a connection to (self, text, world) | Because _____ |

Summary

| Somebody wanted _____ | But _____ | So _____ | Then _____ |

The Effect of an Author's Choice

The author uses...
(choose one)
☐ Vocabulary
☐ Sensory Images
☐ Figurative language
☐ Something else (name it) _____

| An example | Another example |

This creates...
(choose one)
☐ A _____ mood
☐ A _____ feeling
☐ An understating of _____
☐ Something else _____

Examples:

About "The Two Pots"

Structure: The effect of an author's choice

The author uses personification when they have the two pots speak to each other. The two pots "had not gone ten paces before the earthen pot cracked." The author did this in order to give the reader an understanding of how friends sometimes hurt each other like the pots did.

Andrew Beem, teacher

MY Response to "The Two Pots"

Character Feelings

_____ felt	I know because they did	I also know because they said
_____	_____	_____

Earthen pot felt scared when brass pot told him about his plan. I Know because he was not quick to accept the offer. I also know because he said "You know how fragile I am."

— Leia Parker Garcia
Grade 3

Response to "The One-Eyed Doe"

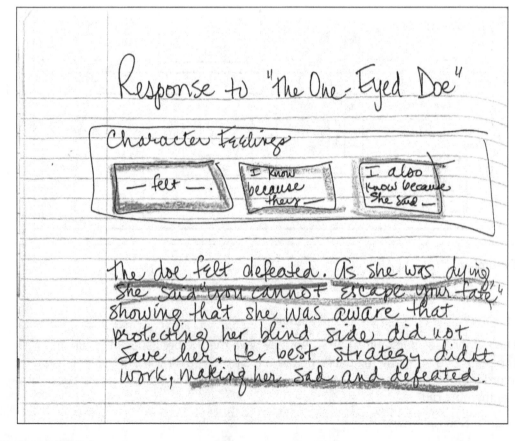

Character Feelings

— felt —.	I know because they —	I also know because she said —

The doe felt defeated. As she was dying she said "you cannot escape your fate," showing that she was aware that protecting her blind side did not save her. Her best strategy didn't work, making her sad and defeated.

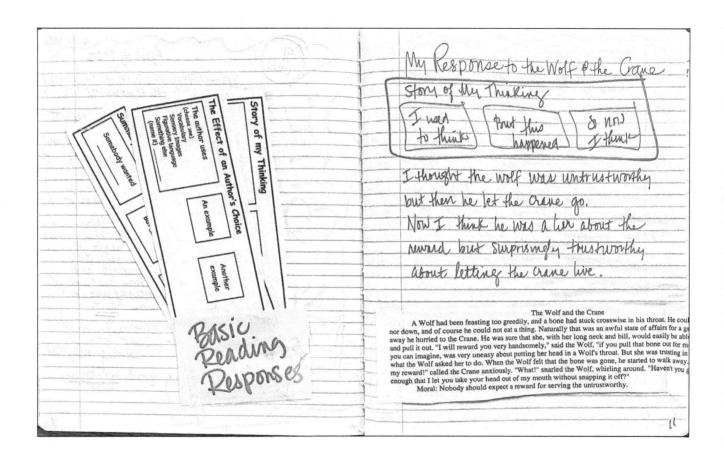

My Response to the Wolf & the Crane

Story of My Thinking

| I used to think | But this happened | So now I think |

I thought the wolf was untrustworthy but then he let the crane go.
Now I think he was a liar about the reward but surprisingly trustworthy about letting the crane live.

The Wolf and the Crane

A Wolf had been feasting too greedily, and a bone had stuck crosswise in his throat. He coul[d] nor down, and of course he could not eat a thing. Naturally that was an awful state of affairs for a g[reedy] away he hurried to the Crane. He was sure that she, with her long neck and bill, would easily be abl[e] and pull it out. "I will reward you very handsomely," said the Wolf, "if you pull that bone out for m[e]" you can imagine, was very uneasy about putting her head in a Wolf's throat. But she was trusting in what the Wolf asked her to do. When the Wolf felt that the bone was gone, he started to walk away[.] my reward!" called the Crane anxiously. "What!" snarled the Wolf, whirling around. "Haven't you g[ot] enough that I let you take your head out of my mouth without snapping it off?"

Moral: Nobody should expect a reward for serving the untrustworthy.

Response to "Diamonds and Toads"

Structure: Effect of an author's Choice

| The author uses | | | The Effect |

The author uses figurative language to reveal character.

The rude daughter "grumbled all the way," showing her bad attitude and resentment.

The narrator also called the her an "ill-bred minx." We saw her as worse than rude.

Tip: Use this process with any text in any genre.

TEACHING NOTE

Our friend Lisa Taiclet shared her process. She introduced one structure each week to her fourth graders. The students taped a copy of the structure to the top of a page. At the end of silent reading time, her fourth graders used one structure each week. After five weeks, they had used all five. From that point on, she let them choose which structure they wanted to use. She said, "It's making for good book discussions since they never all choose the same structure—or even if they do, they notice something different."

STUDENT SAMPLES

The Story of My Thinking: *about Don't Call Me Pruneface!*

    Adyn, Grade 4

I used to think Paul was good as gold but he called Prudence Pruneface so now I know that Paul can be a little mean.

The Story of My Thinking: *about Don't Call Me Pruneface!*

    Braelyn, Grade 4

I used to think that Prudence would never change her ways but once Paul called her Pruneface she realized what it was like to be called names. So now I know that she did change and now Paul and Prudence are friends.

Making a Connection: about *Wonder*

    Kamila, Grade 4

When I read about no one wanting to touch Auggie, I made a connection to the world because in real life, corona [COVID-19 is happening] right now and we can't touch anybody.

Making a Connection: about *The Three Little Wolves and the Big Bad Pig*

    Kamila, Grade 4

When I read about the Big Bad Pig and how cranky he was I made a text-to-self connection because sometimes I'm in a bad mood and do things that seem mean when I should stop and take some deep breaths like the pig did in the end.

Character Feelings: about *Grace for President*

    Mel, Grade 4

Grace felt confused when she heard that there had never been a girl president. I know because she asked the teacher why and made posters for people to vote for her and because she said, "Go vote for a change."

The Effect of an Author's Choice: about *Wonder*

    Mel, Grade 4

The author uses figurative language like when Mr. Tushman said that August "carried up the most hearts." This creates an understanding of how August helped people not judge a book by its cover.

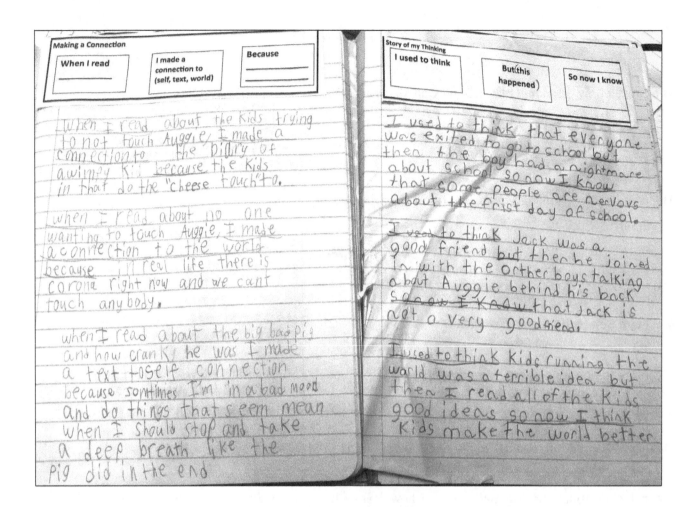

Making a Connection

| When I read _____ | I made a connection to (self, text, world) | Because _____ |

When I read about the kids trying to not touch Auggie, I made a connection to the Diary of a wimpy Kid because the kids in that do the "cheese touch" to.

When I read about no one wanting to touch Auggie, I made a connection to the world because in real life there is corona right now and we cant touch anybody.

When I read about the big bad pig and how cranky he was I made a text to self connection because sometimes I'm in a bad mood and do things that seem mean when I should stop and take a deep breath like the pig did in the end

Story of my Thinking

| I used to think | But (this happened) | So now I know |

I used to think that everyone was exited to go to school but then the boy had a nightmare about school so now I know that some people are nervous about the frist day of school.

I used to think Jack was a good friend but then he joined in with the orther boys talking about Auggie behind his back so now I know that Jack is not a very good friend.

I used to think kids running the world was a terrible idea but then I read all of the kids good ideas so now I think kids make the world better

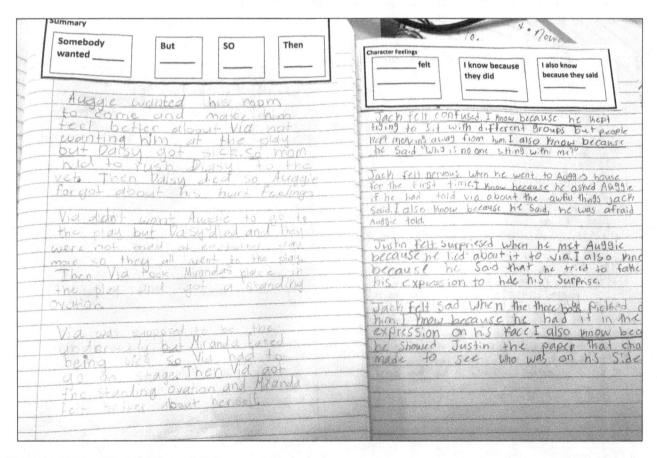

Summary

| Somebody wanted _____ | But | SO | Then |

Auggie wanted his mom to come and make him feel better about Via not wanting him at the play but Daisy got sick so mom had to rush Daisy to the vet. Then Daisy died so Auggie forgot about his hurt feelings.

Via didn't want Auggie to go to the play but Daisy died and they were not mad at eachother any more so they all went to the play. Then Via took Mirandas place in the play and got a standing ovation

Via was supposed to be the under study but Miranda faked being sick so Via had to go on stage. Then Via got the standing ovation and Miranda felt better about herself.

Character Feelings

| _____ felt _____ | I know because they did | I also know because they said |

Jack felt confused I know because he kept trying to sit with different groups but people kept moving away from him. I also know because he said "Why is no one sitting with me?"

Jack felt nervous when he went to Auggie's house for the first time. I know because he asked Auggie if he had told via about the awful things Jack said. I also know because he said, he was afraid Auggie told.

Justin felt surprised when he met Auggie because he lied about it to via. I also know because he said that he tried to fake his expression to hide his Surprise.

Jack felt sad when the three boys picked on him. I know because he had it in the expression on his face. I also know because he showed Justin the paper that cha made to see who was on his side

The Effect of an Author's Choice

The author uses (choose one)
- ☐ Vocabulary
- ☐ Sensory images
- ☐ Figurative language
- ☐ Something else (name it)

an example	another example

This creates (choose one)
- ☐ A _____ mood
- ☐ A _____ feeling
- ☐ An understanding of _____
- ☐ Something else (name it)

The author uses sensory images like Auggie feeling like he was under water and crying the "waterworks." These created an understanding of how scary that night was for Auggie and how poor his hearing is.

The author uses vocabulary like backtracked and singlefire, this creates a visual in my mind of how they searched for the hearing aids.

The author figurative language like a monumental shift and a cosmic shift to give the reader an understanding how big (the

VARIATION

- Let students choose (and copy) a striking line or phrase from their reading.
- Choose a structure from the great lines page.
- Let the structure help you write about your thoughts as you read.
- Read your kernel essay to a partner or group.
- Listen to several other kernel essays.

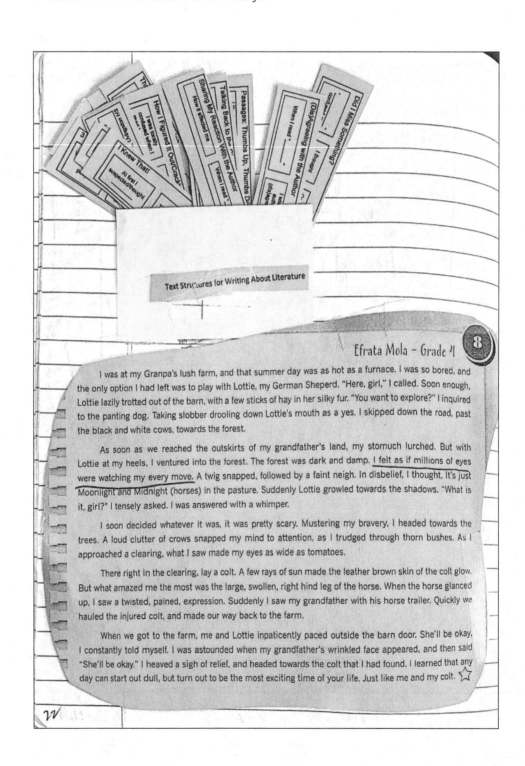

Text Structures for Writing About Literature

Efrata Mola – Grade 4

8

I was at my Granpa's lush farm, and that summer day was as hot as a furnace. I was so bored, and the only option I had left was to play with Lottie, my German Sheperd. "Here, girl," I called. Soon enough, Lottie lazily trotted out of the barn, with a few sticks of hay in her silky fur. "You want to explore?" I inquired to the panting dog. Taking slobber drooling down Lottie's mouth as a yes. I skipped down the road, past the black and white cows, towards the forest.

As soon as we reached the outskirts of my grandfather's land, my stomuch lurched. But with Lottie at my heels, I ventured into the forest. The forest was dark and damp. I felt as if millions of eyes were watching my every move. A twig snapped, followed by a faint neigh. In disbelief, I thought, It's just Moonlight and Midnight (horses) in the pasture. Suddenly Lottie growled towards the shadows. "What is it, girl?" I tensely asked. I was answered with a whimper.

I soon decided whatever it was, it was pretty scary. Mustering my bravery, I headed towards the trees. A loud clutter of crows snapped my mind to attention, as I trudged through thorn bushes. As I approached a clearing, what I saw made my eyes as wide as tomatoes.

There right in the clearing, lay a colt. A few rays of sun made the leather brown skin of the colt glow. But what amazed me the most was the large, swollen, right hind leg of the horse. When the horse glanced up, I saw a twisted, pained, expression. Suddenly I saw my grandfather with his horse trailer. Quickly we hauled the injured colt, and made our way back to the farm.

When we got to the farm, me and Lottie inpaticently paced outside the barn door. She'll be okay, I constantly told myself. I was astounded when my grandfather's wrinkled face appeared, and then said "She'll be okay." I heaved a sigh of relief, and headed towards the colt that I had found. I learned that any day can start out dull, but turn out to be the most exciting time of your life. Just like me and my colt. ☆

Line **"I felt as if millions of eyes were watching my every move."**

structure: clarifier

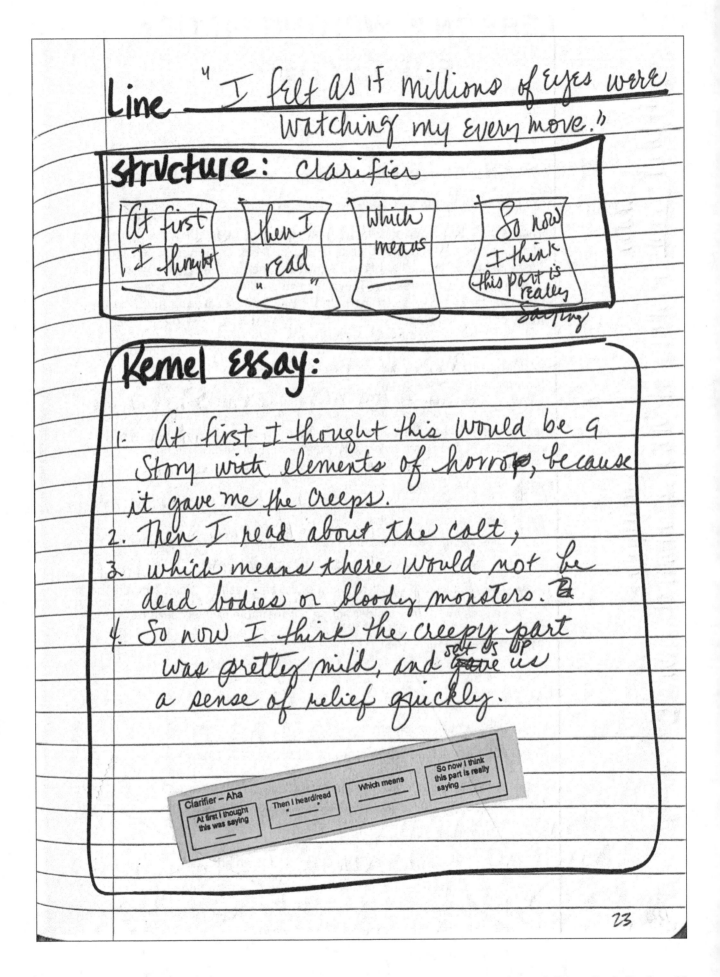

At first I thought	then I read "___"	Which means ___	So now I think this part is really saying

Kernel Essay:

1. At first I thought this would be a story with elements of horror, because it gave me the creeps.
2. Then I read about the colt,
3. which means there would not be dead bodies or bloody monsters.
4. So now I think the creepy part was pretty mild, and set us up gave us a sense of relief quickly.

Clarifier – Aha

At first I thought this was saying ___	Then I heard/read ___	Which means ___	So now I think this part is really saying ___

23

LESSON 2. WRITING FICTION FOR READERS

"We don't have time for fiction-writing in our curriculum. We have to do test prep."

We hear this too often.

There's clearly one fast and reliable way to show students how a writer moves a story along, reveals characters or theme, or evokes a response in a reader, and that is to let the students put on the hat of a writer, write something, and watch what happens when other people hear or read it. They play with adding dialogue to see what the reader understands better or switching point of view and discovering that now their story is funny or heartbreaking.

Being the writer and wielding the writer's tools is the very best kind of preparation for exploring why a writer would do *x*, *y*, or *z* and to gauge what kind of effect that might have on a reader. Besides that, it's fun.

If test prep is the only sellable justification for writing fiction, then we have a practical reason for writing. For other more natural, complex, and fundamentally healthy reasons, read Thomas Newkirk's *Writing Unbound*.

Step 1. Read a fable.

- Read or listen to a fable.
  - You could read more than one fable grouped in the same theme.
  - You could read or listen to a partner read a fable.
- These fables are short; reread it again and again to pick up hidden details.
- You may want to consider acting out the fable to internalize the story.

Step 2. Read the moral.

- What is the moral of the fable?
- Do you agree with the moral? Why or why not?
- Do you believe something else?
- Could there be another moral or lesson to be learned?

Step 3. Write your own version. Pick your approach. Write your own fable based on the fable you read, choosing any of the following:

- Write a sequel to the fable.
- Retell the story as one of the characters (with attitude).
- Rewrite the fable and change the setting (the time, the place).
- Retell this fable in another genre (such as in letter form or as a poem or a journal entry from a character's point of view).
- Change the ending.

Step 4. Choose a text structure. This will help to guide your story and keep it tight.

Step 5. Ask yourself questions. For instance, ask yourself, "If I am writing fiction, have I included the important elements of a plot in my own version?"

- Characters
- Conflict
- Rising action
- Climax
- Falling action
- Resolution

Step 6. Read your story aloud to a partner or group. Listen to theirs, too.

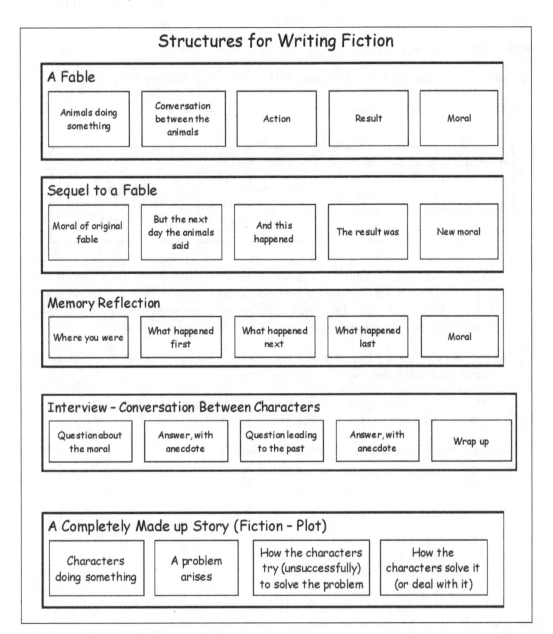

Structures for Writing Fiction

A Fable

| Animals doing something | Conversation between the animals | Action | Result | Moral |

Sequel to a Fable

| Moral of original fable | But the next day the animals said | And this happened | The result was | New moral |

Memory Reflection

| Where you were | What happened first | What happened next | What happened last | Moral |

Interview – Conversation Between Characters

| Question about the moral | Answer, with anecdote | Question leading to the past | Answer, with anecdote | Wrap up |

A Completely Made up Story (Fiction – Plot)

| Characters doing something | A problem arises | How the characters try (unsuccessfully) to solve the problem | How the characters solve it (or deal with it) |

STUDENT SAMPLES

A fable of "The Lion's Share"

Cameron Lamkin, Grade 4

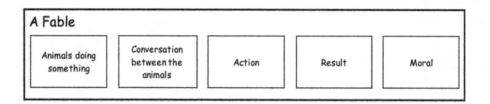

A long time ago, the lion, the fox, the jackal, and I invited each other to go hunting together. I was good with that. Then I ran down a deer, and lion cut it up and gave himself the first piece. (Am I surprised? No.) Just as I was about to claim the next piece, he grabbed the other three. We were all scared to speak.

Moral: Don't hunt with lions.

A Completely Made-Up Story (Fiction Plot) of "The Fox and the Pheasants"

Joaquin Cristian Flores, Grade 7

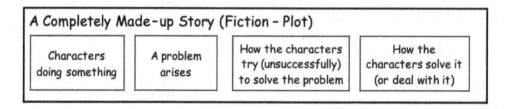

As the day turned to night, we began to gather on the "Great Tree," as we call it. Then into the moonlight slithered a fox. He started to raise himself onto his hind legs and started to . . . dance! I couldn't take my eyes off of him. I couldn't tell if I was in fear of losing sight of him or if I was being hypnotized.

As his dance continued, I began to fall into a daze and I saw everyone was gone. I looked down and there they were . . . on the ground.

The fox then picked them up and ate them. One by one, everyone was then gone. I was then all alone. Lost. Maybe. There I was all by myself.

The fox laughed, then disappeared into the darkness.

Sequel to "The Shipwrecked Impostor"

Arden Allmon, Grade 11

Sequel to a Fable				
Moral of original fable	But the next day the animals said	And this happened	The result was	New moral

The monkey drifted at sea, hoping that another kind soul would be willing to save him from the harsh ocean. He swam and swam trying to find the shore, wishing that he hadn't lied to the kind dolphin who attempted to save him.

Then suddenly, the monkey saw the dolphin again! The dolphin made his way over to the monkey and all the while the monkey apologized for his falsehoods. "I should have never taken advantage of your kindness, and I understand if you don't want to save me again."

"I will save you, **but only** if you promise not to lie. Especially to those who want to help you." The monkey happily agreed and was swooped up by the dolphin to be taken to shore.

As the monkey and the dolphin rode to shore, the monkey knew that lying would never make anything better and might actually hurt himself and others in the end; with this thought, he vowed to never lie again.

3

LESSON 3. WRITING ESSAYS ABOUT THE MORAL

The moral of any fable is a tidy little claim. If we discuss the moral (aloud or in writing), we're examining or building an argument. In examining a moral, students might use any evidence in their experience, in other texts, or in the world's events to

- defend the argument
- take a stand
- analyze the theme
- challenge the claim
- consider attitudes different from their own

Step 1. Read a fable.

- You could read more than one fable grouped in the same theme.
- You could read or listen to a partner read a fable.
- These fables are short; reread it again and again to pick up hidden details.
- You may want to consider acting out the fable to internalize the story.

Step 2. Read the moral.

Moral:

- What is the moral of the fable?

- Do you agree with the moral? Why or why not?

- Do you believe something else?

- Could there be another moral or lesson to be learned?

Step 3. Compose a sentence with your thoughts.

Rainey Wiley, Grade 2   "The Shepherd Boy and the Wolf"

Moral: Liars are not believed, even when they tell the truth.

- What do you think might be true about the moral or lesson in the fable(s)? (We call this a truism.)

- You could start your sentence with "Sometimes . . ."

- Do you believe something else?

- Could there be another moral or lesson to be learned in the fable(s)?

- Compose a sentence orally or write it down. Either way, the thinking work is valuable. Dialogue and conversation are as valuable as making this a writing task.

Step 4. Ask yourself, "How do I know this? What makes me think this is true?"

- Maybe you know it from your own life experience.
- Maybe you know it from a different story or text.
- Maybe you know it because of something happening in world events, whether now or in the past.

Step 5. Choose a text structure from one of the three categories above (life experience, story, world event).

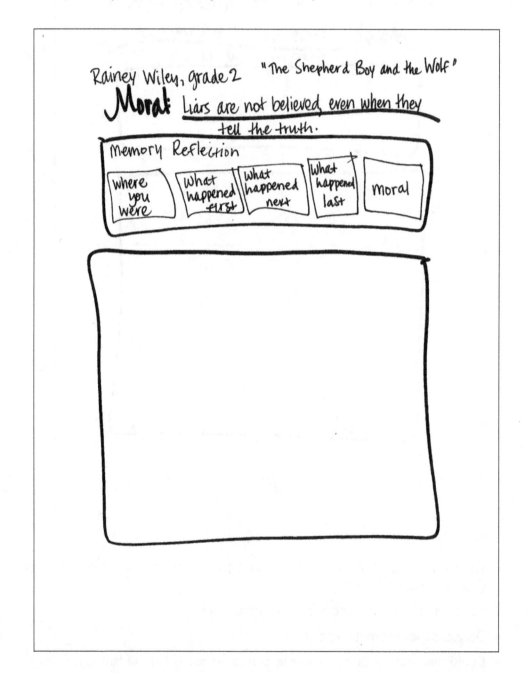

- Write a sentence for each box from your structure.
- Add details to each sentence to turn this kernel essay into a full essay.
  - (For a great way to add details, see Lesson 6 of this book.)

Step 6. Retell or read your short essay to several people.

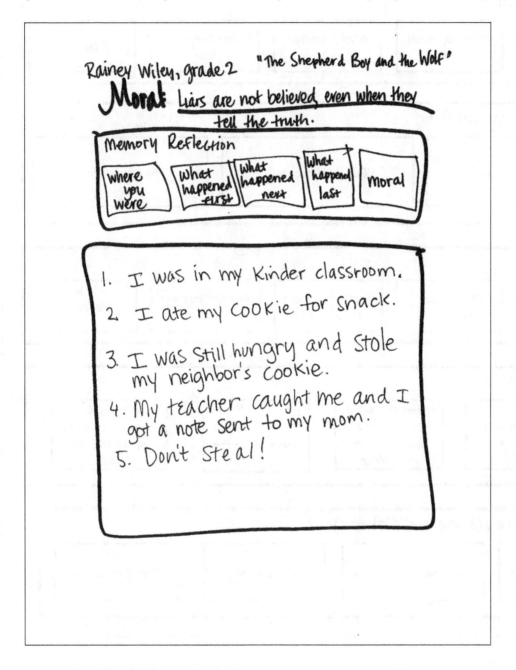

- Listen to their story as well.

TEXT STRUCTURES

Structures for Connecting This to My Life

Memory Reflection

Where you were	What happened first	What happened next	What happened last	Moral

The Story of My Thinking

What I used to think	But this happened	So now I think

My Vignettes

What I think is true	One moment from my life	Another moment from my life	Another moment from my life	I wonder ...

Evolution of a Word

What this word meant to me when I was 4	What this word meant to me when I was a little older	What this word means to me now	What it will probably mean to me when I am older

Comparing Notes (Mine and Others)

Some people think	And other people think	But I think	What that tells me

Structures for Connecting Two Texts

True in Two Fables

Life lesson	How it's true in one fable	How it's true in another fable	I wonder

Book or Movie Connection

Life lesson	How it's true in the fable	How it's true also in a book or movie	I wonder

Character Connection

____ in this fable reminds me of ___ in ____.	One way they are similar	Another way they are similar	What that tells me about the world/me

Compare and Contrast

____ and ____ are very much alike	They both ____ and ____	They are also different in this way	Another way they are different	A new moral (for both)

One Problem, Different Reactions

A problem in the fable	A similar problem in a movie/book/fable	How the character(s) reacted in the 1st text	How the character(s) reacted in the 2nd text	Which one had the better outcome

Structures for World Connections

Current Event Connection

| Life lesson | How it's true in the story | How it's true in a current event | What this tells me |

Historical Event Connection

| Life lesson | How it's true in the story | How it's true in a moment from history | I wonder |

Solving a Problem

| A problem I noticed in the story | This reminds me of a problem in our world | How it was resolved in the story | A possible solution to the current problem |

History of Something

| In the story, _____ reminds me of _____ (moment in history) | When this happened | What people thought then | What people think now |

Curiosity: One Thing You'd Like to Know About

| I have sometimes wondered about | From this story, I know that | From (an event in history or the news), I also know that | But I can't figure out how |

STUDENT SAMPLES

Memory Reflection: "The Shepherd Boy and the Wolf"
Rainey Wiley, Grade 2

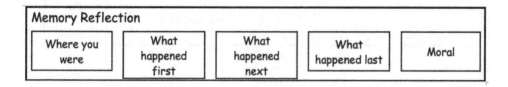

1. I was in my kindergarten classroom.
2. I ate my cookie for snack.
3. I was still hungry and stole my neighbor's cookie.
4. My teacher caught me and I got a note sent to my mom.
5. Don't steal!

One Problem, Different Reactions: "The Father and His Sons"
Callista Gimbel, Grade 5

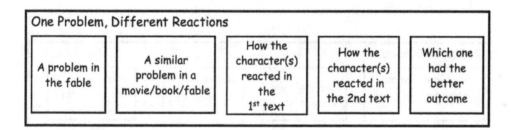

In "The Bremen Town Musicians," all the animals would die or didn't want to work because they were old and weak. They were alone until they met each other, then they worked together.

In "The Father and His Sons," the three sons didn't work together, as in the beginning of the fairytale, "The Bremen Town Musicians."

In the second text, when the brothers didn't work together, they were weak but when they worked together, they were strong and happy. In the "Bremen Town Musicians," they worked together immediately and were happy.

I believe the best outcome was in "The Bremen Town Musicians," as once the animals were together, they stuck together and strived to help even after they achieved their goals.

Historical Event Connection: "The Donkey, the Fox, and the Lion"
Arden Allmon, Grade 11

Historical Event Connection			
Life lesson	How it's true in the story	How it's true in a moment from history	I wonder

1. Loyalty is the most important asset.
2. In the fable, loyalty is proven to be important because if the fox had stayed loyal to the donkey, he wouldn't have been eaten.
3. This reminds me of the American Revolution when Hercules Mulligan was a spy for America on the British troops. While it would have been easy to become a double agent, Mulligan stayed loyal and helped America win the war. Loyalty won!
4. I wonder what would have happened to the fox if he had stayed loyal to his friend and didn't try to sell his friend out.

Character Connection: "The Gnat and the Bull"
Kayla Hosny, Grade 12

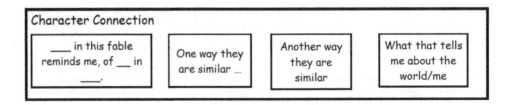

Character Connection			
____ in this fable reminds me, of ___ in ____.	One way they are similar ...	Another way they are similar	What that tells me about the world/me

1. The gnat in this fable reminds me of Hamlet in *Hamlet.*
2. One way they are similar is they both are very pensive about meaningless things. They both tend to think about subjects that don't matter, subjects that other people don't think about.
3. Another way they are similar is that they seem unaware of their arrogance. They pass it off as conscientiousness when really it is their own image they are concerned about. In Hamlet's case, he even has a morbid countenance and acts sorrowful while all the time being self-absorbed.
4. This tells me about the world and me that when we act certain ways, claiming we care and are concerned about others, a lot of times we are only interested in our own image and good reputation. We must check our heart to see if we are acting the way we are acting only because of self-gain or pride.

Tip: Add a sketch or photo to illustrate your thinking.

Extension: You or your students might create new structures.

The Miser

A miser had buried his gold in a secret place in his garden. Every day, he went to the spot, dug up the treasure, and counted it piece by piece to make sure it was all there. He made so many trips that a thief, who had been observing him, guessed what it was the miser had hidden and, one night, quietly dug up the treasure and made off with it.

When the miser discovered his loss, he was overcome with grief and despair. He groaned and cried and tore his hair. A passerby heard his cries and asked what had happened. "My gold! O my gold!" cried the miser, wildly. "Someone has robbed me!"

"Your gold! There in that hole? Why did you put it there? Why did you not keep it in the house where you could easily get it when you had to buy things?"

"Buy!" screamed the miser angrily. "Why, I never touched the gold. I couldn't think of spending any of it."

The stranger picked up a large stone and threw it into the hole. "If that is the case," he said, "cover up that stone. It is worth just as much to you as the treasure you lost!"

Moral: A possession is worth no more than the use we make of it.

The Donkey and His Shadow

A traveler had hired a donkey to carry him to a distant part of the country. The owner of the donkey went with the traveler, walking beside him to drive the donkey and point out the way. The road led across a treeless plain where the sun beat down fiercely. So intense did the heat become that the traveler at last decided to stop for a rest, and as there was no other shade to be found, the traveler sat down in the shadow of the donkey. Now the heat had affected the driver as much as it had the traveler and even more, for he had been walking. Wishing also to rest in the shade cast by the donkey, he began to quarrel with the traveler, saying he had hired the donkey and not the shadow it cast. The two soon came to blows, and while they were fighting, the donkey took to its heels.

Moral: In quarreling about the shadow, we often lose the substance.

The Goose With the Golden Eggs

There was once a countryman who possessed the most wonderful goose you can imagine, for every day when he visited the nest, the goose had laid a beautiful, glittering, golden egg. The countryman took the eggs to market and soon began to get rich. But it was not long before he grew impatient with the goose because she gave him only a single golden egg a day. He was not getting rich fast enough. Then one day, after he had finished counting his money, the idea came to him that he could get all the golden eggs at once by killing the goose and cutting it open. But when the deed was done, not a single golden egg did he find, and his precious goose was dead.

Moral: Those who have plenty want more and so lose all they have.

The Fisherman and the Little Fish

A poor fisherman, who lived on the fish he caught, had bad luck one day and caught nothing but a very small fry.

The fisherman was about to put it in his basket when the little fish said, "Please spare me, Mr. Fisherman! I am so small it is not worthwhile to carry me home. When I am bigger, I shall make you a much better meal."

But the fisherman quickly put the fish into his basket. "How foolish I should be," he said, "to throw you back. However small you may be, you are better than nothing at all."

Moral: A small gain is worth more than a large promise.

The Woman and Her Hen

A woman had a hen that laid an egg every day. The fowl was of a superior breed, and the eggs were very fine and sold for a good price. The woman thought that by giving the hen double as much food as she had been in the habit of giving her, the bird might be brought to lay two eggs a day instead of one. So the quantity of food was doubled accordingly, and the hen grew very fat and quit laying altogether.

Moral: Greediness may override itself.

The Shepherd Boy and the Wolf

A shepherd boy tended his master's sheep near a dark forest not far from the village. Soon, he found life in the pasture very dull. All he could do to amuse himself was talk to his dog or play on his shepherd's pipe. One day, as he sat watching the sheep and the quiet forest and thinking what he would do should he see a wolf, he thought of a plan to amuse himself. His master had told him to call for help should a wolf attack the flock, and the villagers would drive it away. So now, though he had not seen anything that even looked like a wolf, he ran toward the village shouting at the top of his voice, "Wolf! Wolf!"

As he expected, the villagers who heard the cry dropped their work and ran in great excitement to the pasture. But when they got there, they found the boy doubled up with laughter at the trick he had played on them. A few days later, the shepherd boy again shouted, "Wolf! Wolf!" Again, the villagers ran to help him, only to be laughed at again.

Then one evening as the sun was setting behind the forest and the shadows were creeping out over the pasture, a wolf really did spring from the underbrush and fall upon the sheep. In terror, the boy ran toward the village shouting, "Wolf! Wolf!" But though the villagers heard the cry, they did not run to help him as they had before.

"He cannot fool us again," they said. The wolf killed a great many of the boy's sheep and then slipped away into the forest.

Moral: Liars are not believed, even when they speak the truth.

The Donkey in the Lion's Skin

A donkey found a lion's skin left in the forest by a hunter. He dressed himself in it and amused himself by hiding in a thicket and rushing out suddenly at the animals who passed that way. All took to their heels the moment they saw him. The donkey was so pleased to see the animals running away from him, just as if he were King Lion himself, that he could not keep from expressing his delight by a loud, harsh bray. A fox, who ran with the rest, stopped short as soon as he heard the voice. Approaching the donkey, he said with a laugh, "If you had kept your mouth shut, you might have frightened me, too. But you gave yourself away with that silly bray."

Moral: A fool may deceive by his dress and appearance, but his words will soon show what he really is.

Mercury and the Woodman

A poor woodman was cutting down a tree near the edge of a deep pool in the forest. It was late in the day and the woodman was tired. He had been working since sunrise and his strokes were not as sure as they had been early that morning. Thus it happened that the axe slipped and flew out of his hands into the pool. The woodman was in despair. The axe was all he possessed with which to make a living, and he had not money enough to buy a new one. As he stood wringing his hands and weeping, the god Mercury suddenly appeared and asked what the trouble was. The woodman told what had happened, and straightway the kind Mercury dived into the pool. When he came up again, he held a wonderful golden axe.

"Is this your axe?" Mercury asked the woodman.

"No," answered the honest woodman, "that is not my axe."

Mercury laid the golden axe on the bank and sprang back into the pool. This time, he brought up an axe of silver, but the woodman declared again that his axe was just an ordinary one with a wooden handle. Mercury dived down for the third time, and when he came up again, he had the very axe that had been lost. The poor woodman was very glad that his axe had been found and could not thank the kind god enough.

"I admire your honesty," Mercury said, "and as a reward, you may have all three axes, the gold and the silver as well as your own."

The happy woodman returned to his home with his treasures, and soon the story of his good fortune was known to everybody in the village. Now there were several woodmen in the village who believed that they could easily win the same good fortune. They hurried out into the woods—one here, one there—and, hiding their axes in the bushes, pretended they had lost them. Then they wept and wailed and called on Mercury to help them. And indeed, Mercury did appear, first to this one, then to that one. To each one he showed an axe of gold, and each one eagerly claimed it to be the one he had lost. But Mercury did not give them the golden axe. Oh no! Instead, he gave them each a hard whack over the head with it and sent them home. And when they returned next day to look for their own axes, they were nowhere to be found.

Moral: Honesty is always best.

The Shipwrecked Impostor

The shipwrecked chimpanzee had been clinging for a long time to a piece of wood when a dolphin came up and offered to carry him ashore. This kind proposition was immediately accepted, and as they moved along, the chimp commenced to tell the fish many marvelous tales, every one of them a bundle of falsehoods.

"Well, well, you are indeed an educated chap," said the dolphin in admiration. "My schooling has been sadly neglected, as I went to sea when I was but a week old."

Just then they entered a large bay and the dolphin, referring to a path there, said, "I suppose you know Herring Roads?"

The chimp, taking this for the name of a fellow and not wishing to appear ignorant, replied, "Do I know Rhodes? Well, I should almost think so! He's an old college chum of mine, and related to our family by—" This was too much for the dolphin, who immediately made a great leap and then, diving quickly, left the impostor in the air for an instant before he splashed back and disappeared.

Moral: A liar deceives only himself.

The Thief and the Innkeeper

A thief hired a room in a tavern and stayed a while in the hope of stealing something that should enable him to pay his reckoning. When he had waited some days in vain, he saw the innkeeper dressed in a new and handsome coat and sitting before his door. The thief sat down beside him and talked with him. As the conversation began to flag, the thief yawned terribly and, at the same time, howled like a wolf. The innkeeper said, "Why do you howl so fearfully?"

"I will tell you," said the thief, "but first let me ask you to hold my clothes, or I shall tear them to pieces. If I yawn for the third time, I actually turn into a wolf and attack men."

With this speech, he commenced a second fit of yawning and again howled like a wolf, as he had the first. The innkeeper, believing what he said, became greatly alarmed and, rising from his seat, attempted to run away. The thief laid hold of his coat, yawned a third time, and set up a terrible howl. The innkeeper, frightened lest he should be attacked, left his new coat in the thief's hand and ran as fast as he could into the inn for safety. The thief made off with the coat and did not return again to the inn.

Moral: Not every tale is to be believed.

The Flies and the Honey

A jar of honey was upset and the sticky sweetness flowed out on the table. The sweet smell of the honey soon brought a large number of flies buzzing around. They did not wait for an invitation. No, indeed; they settled right down, feet and all, to gorge themselves. The flies were quickly smeared from head to foot with honey. Their wings stuck together. They could not pull their feet out of the sticky mass. And so they died for a taste of sweetness.

Moral: Greed can be destructive.

The Wolf, the Goat, and the Kid

Mother Goat was going to market one morning to get provisions for her household, which consisted of but one little kid and herself. "Take good care of the house, my son," she said to the kid as she carefully latched the door. "Do not let anyone in, unless he gives you this password: 'Down with the wolf!'"

Strangely enough, a wolf was lurking near and heard what the goat had said. So as soon as Mother Goat was out of sight, up he trotted to the door and knocked. "Down with the wolf," said the wolf softly. It was the right password, but when the kid peeped through a crack in the door and saw the shadowy figure outside, he did not feel at all easy.

"Show me a white paw," he said, "or I won't let you in." A white paw, of course, is a feature few wolves can show, and so Master Wolf had to go away as hungry as he had come. "You can never be too sure," said the kid when he saw the wolf making off to the woods.

Moral: Two pieces of evidence are better than one.

The Tortoise and the Eagle

A tortoise, basking in the sun, wondered aloud what it would be like to fly. An eagle, overhearing her, offered to take her aloft. The tortoise agreed and the eagle carried her almost to the clouds but suddenly let her go. She fell to the ground, dashing her shell to pieces. The eagle then landed and made a meal of the poor tortoise.

Moral: You should never put yourself in your enemy's clutches.

The Lion, the Fox, and the Beasts

The lion once gave out that he was sick unto death and summoned the animals to come and hear his last will and testament. So the fox came to the lion's cave and stopped there, listening for a long time. He watched a sheep go in and, before she came out, a calf came up to receive the last wishes of the lord of the beasts. But soon, the lion seemed to recover and came to the mouth of his cave; he saw the fox, who had been waiting outside for some time.

"Why did you not come to pay your respects to me?" said the lion to the fox.

"I beg your Majesty's pardon," said the fox, "but I noticed the track of the animals that have already come to you; and while I see many hoof-marks going in, I see none coming out. Till the animals that have entered your cave come out again, I prefer to remain in the open air."

Moral: Observing your surroundings can keep you safe.

The Fox and the Ape

Upon the death of the lion, the beasts of the forest assembled to choose another king. The ape played so many grimaces, gambols, and antics that he was elected by a large majority and the crown was placed upon his head. The fox was envious of this distinction. Soon after, the fox saw a trap baited with a piece of meat. He approached the new king and said with mock humility, "May it please your majesty, I have found a treasure to which, if you will deign to accompany me, I will guide you." The ape set off with the fox and, on arriving at the spot, laid his paw upon the meat. Snap! went the trap and caught him by the fingers. Mad with shame and pain, he reproached the fox for being a traitor. The fox laughed heartily and, going off, said over his shoulder with a sneer, "You call yourself a king and don't understand a trap!"

Moral: Popularity doesn't make a person competent for every job.

The Swan and the Goose

A certain rich man bought a goose and a swan in the market. He fed the one for his table and kept the other for the sake of its song. When the time came for killing the goose, the cook went to get him at night, when it was dark; he was not able to distinguish one bird from the other. By mistake, he caught the swan instead of the goose. The swan, threatened with death, burst forth into song and thus made himself known by his voice and preserved his life by his melody.

Moral: A person does better when they use their own talents.

The Town Mouse and the Country Mouse

A town mouse once visited a relative who lived in the country. For lunch, the country mouse served wheat stalks, roots, and acorns, with a dash of cold water for drink. The town mouse ate very sparingly, nibbling a little of this and a little of that, making it very plain by her manner that she ate the simple food only to be polite. After the meal, the friends had a long talk—or rather, the town mouse talked about her life in the city while the country mouse listened. They then went to bed in a cozy nest in the hedgerow and slept in quiet and comfort until morning. In her sleep, the country mouse dreamed she was a town mouse with all the luxuries and delights of city life that her friend had described for her. So the next day, when the town mouse asked the country mouse to go home with her to the city, she gladly said yes. When they reached the mansion in which the town mouse lived, they found on the table in the dining room the leavings of a very fine banquet. There were sweetmeats and jellies, pastries, delicious cheeses—indeed, the most tempting foods that a mouse can imagine. But just as the country mouse was about to nibble a dainty bit of pastry, she heard a cat mew loudly and scratch at the door. In great fear. the mice scurried to a hiding place, where they lay quite still for a long time, hardly daring to breathe. When at last they ventured back to the feast, the door opened suddenly and in came the servants to clear the table, followed by the house dog. The country mouse stopped in the town mouse's den only long enough to pick up her carpet bag and umbrella. "You may have luxuries and dainties that I have not," she said as she hurried away, "but I prefer my plain food and simple life in the country with the peace and security that go with it."

Moral: A simple life can be as rewarding as a sophisticated life.

The Gnat and the Bull

A gnat flew over the meadow with much buzzing for so small a creature and settled on the tip of one of the horns of a bull. After he had rested a short time, he made ready to fly away. But before he left, he begged the bull's pardon for having used his horn for a resting place. "You must be very glad to have me go now," he said.

"It's all the same to me," replied the bull. "I did not even know you were there."

Moral: We are often of greater importance in our own eyes than in the eyes of our neighbor.

The Huntsman and the Fisherman

A huntsman, returning with his dogs from the field, fell in by chance with a fisherman who was bringing home a basket well laden with fish. The huntsman wished to have the fish, and their owner experienced an equal longing for the contents of the game bag. They quickly agreed to exchange the produce of their day's sport. Each was so well pleased with his bargain that they made for some time the same exchange day after day. Finally, a neighbor said to them, "If you go on in this way, you will soon destroy by frequent use the pleasure of your exchange, and each will again wish to retain the fruits of his own sport."

Moral: Variety makes life better.

The North Wind and the Sun

The north wind and the sun had a quarrel about which of them was the stronger. While they were disputing with much heat and bluster, a traveler passed along the road wrapped in a cloak. "Let us agree," said the sun, "that he who is stronger can strip that traveler of his cloak."

"Very well," growled the north wind, and at once sent a cold, howling blast against the traveler. With the first gust of wind, the ends of the cloak whipped about the traveler's body. But he immediately wrapped it closely around him, and the harder the wind blew, the tighter he held it to him. The north wind tore angrily at the cloak, but all his efforts were in vain.

Then the sun began to shine. At first his beams were gentle, and in the pleasant warmth after the bitter cold of the north wind, the traveler unfastened his cloak and let it hang loosely from his shoulders. The sun's rays grew warmer and warmer. The man took off his cap and mopped his brow. At last, he became so heated that he pulled off his cloak and, to escape the blazing sunshine, threw himself down in the welcome shade of a tree by the roadside.

Moral: Gentleness and kind persuasion win where force and bluster fail.

The Fox and the Stork

The fox one day thought of a plan to amuse himself at the expense of the stork, at whose odd appearance he was always laughing. "You must come and dine with me today," he said to the stork, smiling to himself at the trick he was going to play. The stork gladly accepted the invitation and arrived in good time and with a very good appetite. For dinner, the fox served soup. But it was set out in a very shallow dish, and all the stork could do was to wet the very tip of his bill. Not a drop of soup could he get. But the fox lapped it up easily and, to increase the disappointment of the stork, made a great show of enjoyment. The hungry stork was much displeased at the trick, but he was a calm, even-tempered fellow and saw no good in flying into a rage. Instead, not long afterward, he invited the fox to dine with him in turn. The fox arrived promptly and the stork served a fish dinner that had an appetizing smell. But it was served in a tall jar with a very narrow neck. The stork could easily get at the food with his long bill, but all the fox could do was to lick the outside of the jar and sniff at the delicious fragrance.

Moral: A person who plays tricks on others should be ready for the same treatment.

The Lion's Share

A long time ago, the lion, the fox, the jackal, and the wolf agreed to go hunting together, sharing with each other whatever they found. One day, the wolf ran down a stag and immediately called his comrades to divide the spoil. Without being asked, the lion placed himself at the head of the feast to do the carving and, with a great show of fairness, began to count the guests. "One," he said, counting on his claws, "that is myself the lion. Two, that's the wolf; three is the jackal; and the fox makes four." He then very carefully divided the stag into four equal parts. "I am king," he said when he had finished, "so of course I get the first part. This next part falls to me because I am the strongest; and this is mine because I am the bravest." He now began to glare at the others very savagely. "If any of you have any claim to the part that is left," he growled, stretching his claws menacingly, "now is the time to speak up."

Moral: The strongest person usually gets their way.

The Monkeys and Their Mother

The monkey, it is said, has two young ones at each birth. The mother cuddles one and nurtures it with the greatest affection and care but hates and neglects the other. It happened once that the young one that was caressed and loved was smothered by the too-great affection of the mother, while the despised one was nurtured and reared in spite of the neglect to which it was exposed.

Moral: The best intentions will not always ensure success.

The Horse, the Hunter, and the Stag

A quarrel had arisen between the horse and the stag, so the horse came to a hunter to ask for his help in taking revenge on the stag. The hunter agreed but said, "If you desire to conquer the stag, you must permit me to place this piece of iron between your jaws so that I may guide you with these reins and allow this saddle to be placed upon your back so that I may keep steady upon you as we follow after the enemy."

The horse agreed to the conditions, and the hunter soon saddled and bridled him. Then with the aid of the hunter, the horse soon overcame the stag. He said to the hunter, "Now, get off, and remove these things from my mouth and back."

"Not so fast, friend," said the hunter. "I have now got you under bit and spur and prefer to keep you as you are at present."

Moral: Once you give something up, you may never get it back.

The Donkey, the Fox, and the Lion

A donkey and a fox had become close comrades and were constantly in each other's company. While the donkey cropped a fresh bit of greens, the fox would devour a chicken from the neighboring farmyard or a bit of cheese filched from the dairy. One day, the pair unexpectedly met a lion. The donkey was very much frightened, but the fox calmed his fears. "I will talk to him," he said. So the fox walked boldly up to the lion. "Your highness," he said in a low voice so the donkey could not hear him. "I've got a fine scheme in my head. If you promise not to hurt me, I will lead that foolish creature yonder into a pit where he can't get out, and you can feast at your pleasure." The lion agreed and the fox returned to the donkey. "I made him promise not to hurt us," said the fox. "But come, I know a good place to hide till he is gone." So the fox led the donkey into a deep pit. But when the lion saw that the donkey was his for the taking, he first struck down the traitor fox.

Moral: It never works out to betray a friend.

The Serpent and the Eagle

A serpent had succeeded in surprising an eagle and had wrapped himself around the eagle's neck. The eagle could reach the serpent neither with beak nor claws. Far into the sky he soared, trying to shake off his enemy. But the serpent's hold only tightened, and slowly the eagle sank back to earth, gasping for breath. A countryman chanced to see the unequal combat. In pity for the noble eagle, he rushed up and soon had loosened the coiling serpent and freed the eagle. The serpent was furious. He had no chance to bite the watchful countryman. Instead, he struck at the drinking horn hanging at the countryman's belt and let the poison of his fangs fly into it. The countryman now went on toward home. Becoming thirsty on the way, he filled his horn at a spring and was about to drink. There was a sudden rush of great wings. Sweeping down, the eagle seized the poisoned horn from out of his savior's hands and flew away with it to hide it where it could never be found.

Moral: An act of kindness is well repaid.

The Two Pots

Two pots, one of brass and the other of clay, stood together on the hearthstone. One day, the brass pot proposed to the earthen pot that they go out into the world together. But the earthen pot excused himself, saying that it would be wiser for him to stay in the corner by the fire. "It would take so little to break me," he said. "You know how fragile I am. The least shock is sure to shatter me!"

"Don't let that keep you at home," urged the brass pot. "I shall take very good care of you. If we should happen to meet anything hard, I will step between and save you." So the earthen pot at last consented, and the two set out side by side, jolting along on three stubby legs first to this side, then to that, bumping into each other at every step. The earthen pot could not survive that sort of companionship very long. They had not gone ten paces before the earthen pot cracked; at the next jolt, he flew into a thousand pieces.

Moral: Friends can accidently hurt one another.

The Belly and the Members

One day it occurred to the members of the body that they were doing all the work while the belly had all the food. So they held a meeting and decided to strike until the belly consented to its proper share of the work. The hands refused to take the food, the mouth refused to receive it, and the teeth had no work to do. After a day or two, the members began to find that they themselves were in poor condition: The hands could hardly move, the mouth was parched and dry, and the legs were unable to support the rest. Thus they found that even the belly was doing necessary work for the body, and they all must work together or the body will go to pieces.

Moral: When members of a team withdraw support, everyone suffers.

The Wolf and the Crane

A wolf had been feasting too greedily and a bone had gotten stuck crosswise in his throat. He could get it neither up nor down, and of course, he could not eat a thing. Naturally, that was an awful state of affairs for a greedy wolf. So away he hurried to the crane. He was sure that she, with her long neck and bill, would easily be able to reach the bone and pull it out. "I will reward you very handsomely," said the wolf, "if you pull that bone out for me." The crane, as you can imagine, was very uneasy about putting her head in a wolf's throat. But she was trusting in nature, so she did what the wolf asked her to do. When the wolf felt that the bone was gone, he started to walk away.

"But what about my reward?" called the crane anxiously.

"What?" snarled the wolf, whirling around. "Haven't you got it? Isn't it enough that I let you take your head out of my mouth without snapping it off?"

Moral: Nobody should expect a reward for serving the untrustworthy.

The Dove and the Ant

An ant went to the bank of a river to quench its thirst and was carried away by the rush of the stream, nearly drowning. A dove, sitting on a tree overhanging the water, plucked a leaf and let it fall into the stream close to the ant. The ant climbed onto it and floated in safety to the bank. Shortly afterward, a bird hunter came and stood under the tree and laid his trap for the dove, which sat in the branches. The ant, perceiving his design, stung the hunter in the foot. In pain, the bird hunter threw down the twigs, and the noise made the dove take wing.

Moral: A grateful heart will find an opportunity to show appreciation.

The Lion and the Donkey

One day as the lion walked proudly down a forest aisle and the animals respectfully made way for him, a donkey brayed a scornful remark as he passed. The lion felt a flash of anger. But when he turned his head and saw who had spoken, he walked quietly on. He would not honor the fool with even so much as a stroke of his claws.

Moral: Nobody is too strong or too good to avoid criticism.

The Monkey and the Cat

Once upon a time, a cat and a monkey lived as pets in the same house. They were great friends and were constantly in all sorts of mischief together. What they seemed to think of more than anything else was to get something to eat, and it did not matter much to them how they got it. One day they were sitting by the fire, watching some chestnuts roasting on the hearth. How to get them was the question. "I would gladly get them," said the cunning monkey, "but you are much more skillful at such things than I am. Pull them out and I'll divide them between us." The cat stretched out her paw very carefully, pushed aside some of the cinders, and drew back her paw very quickly. Then she tried it again, this time pulling a chestnut half out of the fire. A third time and she drew out the chestnut. She went through this performance several times, each time singeing her paw severely. As fast as she pulled the chestnuts out of the fire, the monkey ate them up. Now the master came in and the rascals scampered away, leaving Mistress Cat with a burnt paw and no chestnuts. From that time on, they say, she contented herself with mice and rats and had little to do with Sir Monkey.

Moral: Selfishness can ruin a friendship.

The Donkey Carrying the Image

A sacred image was being carried to the temple. It was mounted on a donkey adorned with garlands and gorgeous trappings, and a grand procession of priests and pages followed it through the streets. As the donkey walked along, the people bowed their heads reverently or fell on their knees, and the donkey thought the honor was being paid to himself. With his head full of this foolish idea, he became so puffed up with pride and vanity that he halted and started to bray loudly. But in the midst of his song, his driver guessed what the donkey had got into his head and began to beat him unmercifully with a stick. "Go along with you, you stupid donkey," he cried. "The honor is not meant for you but for the image you are carrying."

Moral: People should not take credit that is due to others.

The Peacock and the Crane

A peacock, puffed up with vanity, met a crane one day and, to impress him, spread his gorgeous tail in the sun. "Look," he said. "What have you to compare with this? I am dressed in all the glory of the rainbow, while your feathers are gray as dust!"

The crane spread his broad wings and flew up toward the sun. "Follow me if you can," he said. But the peacock stood where he was among the birds of the barnyard while the crane soared in freedom far up into the blue sky.

Moral: The useful is more valuable than the ornamental.

The Horse and the Groom

A dishonest groom regularly sold half of the oats that were daily allowed for a horse, the care of which was entrusted to him. He would, however, keep brushing the animal's coat for hours to make him appear in good condition. The horse naturally resented this treatment. "If you really wish me to look sleek," said he, "then in the future, give me half the currying and leave off selling half my food."

Moral: A person can hide bad deeds behind good appearances.

The Boys and the Frogs

Some boys were playing one day at the edge of a pond in which lived a family of frogs. The boys amused themselves by throwing stones into the pond to make them skip on top of the water. The stones were flying thick and fast and the boys were enjoying themselves very much; but the poor frogs in the pond were trembling with fear. At last one of the frogs, the oldest and bravest, put his head out of the water and said, "Oh, please, dear children, stop your cruel play! Though it may be fun for you, it means death to us!"

Moral: One person's fun should not cause another person's unhappiness.

The Fox and the Grapes

A fox one day spied a beautiful bunch of ripe grapes hanging from a vine trained along the branches of a tree. The grapes seemed ready to burst with juice, and the fox's mouth watered as he gazed longingly at them. The bunch hung from a high branch, and the fox had to jump for it. The first time he jumped, he missed it by a long way. So he walked off a short distance and took a running leap at it, only to fall short once more. Again and again he tried, but in vain. He sat down and looked at the grapes in disgust. "What a fool I am," he said. "Here I am wearing myself out to get a bunch of sour grapes that are not worth gaping for." And off he walked very, very scornfully.

Moral: There are many who pretend to despise and belittle that which is beyond their reach.

The Raven and the Swan

A raven, which you know is black as coal, was envious of the swan because her feathers were as white as the purest snow. The foolish bird got the idea that if he lived like the swan, swimming and diving all day long and eating the weeds and plants that grow in the water, his feathers would turn white like the swan's. So he left his home in the woods and fields and flew down to live on the lakes and in the marshes. But though he washed and washed all day long, almost drowning himself at it, his feathers remained as black as ever. And as the water weeds he ate did not agree with him, he got thinner and thinner and at last, he died.

Moral: A change of habits will not alter nature.

The Geese and the Cranes

The geese and the cranes were feeding in the same meadow when a bird hunter came to ensnare them in his nets. The cranes, being light of wing, fled away at his approach while the geese, being slower of flight and heavier in their bodies, were captured.

Moral: Life isn't always fair.

The Hares and the Frogs

Hares, as you know, are very timid. The least shadow sends them scurrying in fright to a hiding place. One day, they passed a pond where a family of frogs was sitting among the reeds on the bank. In an instant, the startled frogs were seeking safety in the mud. "Look," cried a hare. "Things are not so bad after all, for here are creatures who are even afraid of us!"

Moral: However unfortunate we may think we are, there is always someone worse off than ourselves.

The Hen and the Swallow

A hen, finding the eggs of a viper and carefully keeping them warm, nourished them into life. A swallow, observing what she had done, said, "You silly creature! Why have you hatched these vipers which, when they shall have grown, will inflict injury on all, beginning with yourself?"

Moral: Acts of kindness can sometimes backfire.

The Donkey, the Rooster, and the Lion

A donkey and a rooster lived in a farmyard together. One day, a hungry lion passed by and, seeing the donkey in good condition, resolved to make a meal of him. Now, they say that there is nothing a lion hates so much as the crowing of a rooster, and at that moment, the rooster happened to crow. The lion straightway made off with all haste from the spot. The donkey, mightily amused to think that a lion should be frightened at a bird, plucked up the courage and galloped after him, delighted with the notion of driving the king of beasts before him. He had, however, gone no great distance when the lion turned sharply round upon him and made an end of him.

Moral: Pride can end in ruin.

The Dogs and the Hides

Some hungry dogs saw a number of hides at the bottom of a stream where the tanner had put them to soak. A fine hide makes an excellent meal for a hungry dog, but the water was deep and the dogs could not reach the hides from the bank. So they held a council and decided that the very best thing to do was to drink up the river. All fell to lapping up the water as fast as they could. They drank and drank until, one after another, all of them burst with drinking. Still, for all their effort, the water in the river remained as high as ever.

Moral: It's always wise to know what you can handle.

The Raven and the Snake

A hungry raven, searching for prey, came across a snake lying at full length on a sunny bank. He seized him in his long beak and would have devoured him, but the snake, twisting and turning about, bit the raven with his venomous fangs so that he died in great pain.

Moral: It is wrong to satisfy your appetite at the expense of another's welfare.

The Cat and the Mice

A certain house was overrun with mice. A cat, discovering this, made her way into it and began to catch and eat them one by one. Fearing for their lives, the mice kept themselves close in their holes. The cat was no longer able to get at them and perceived that she must tempt them forth by some device. For this purpose, she jumped upon a peg and, suspending herself from it, pretended to be dead. One of the mice, peeping out, saw her in that position and said, "Ah, my good madam, we will not come near you. It is wisest to keep a safe distance."

Moral: It is foolish to put yourself at the mercy of a known enemy.

The Shepherd and the Sheep

A shepherd driving his sheep to a wood saw an oak of unusual size full of acorns so, spreading his cloak under the branches, he climbed up into the tree and shook them down. The sheep eating the acorns inadvertently frayed and tore the cloak. When the shepherd came down and saw what was done, he said, "O you most ungrateful creatures! You provide wool to make garments for all other men but you destroy the clothes of him who feeds you."

Moral: Hunger can lead to destruction.

The Frogs Asking for a King

The frogs were tired of governing themselves. They had so much freedom that it had spoiled them, and they did nothing but sit around croaking in a bored manner and wishing for a government that could entertain them with the pomp and display of royalty and rule them in a way to make them know they were being ruled. No milk and water government for them, they declared. So they sent a petition to Jupiter asking for a king. Jupiter saw what simple and foolish creatures they were, but to keep them quiet and make them think they had a king, he threw down a huge log, which fell into the water with a great splash. The frogs hid themselves among the reeds and grasses, thinking the new king to be some fearful giant. But they soon discovered how tame and peaceable King Log was. In a short time, the younger frogs were using him for a diving platform while the older frogs made him a meeting place where they complained loudly to Jupiter about the government. To teach the frogs a lesson, the ruler of the gods now sent a crane to be king of Frogland. The crane proved to be a very different sort of king from old King Log. He gobbled up the poor frogs right and left and they soon saw what fools they had been. In mournful croaks, they begged Jupiter to take away the cruel tyrant before they should all be destroyed. "How now!" cried Jupiter. "Are you not yet content? You have what you asked for and so you have only yourselves to blame for your misfortunes."

Moral: It's important to consider the outcome when asking for change.

The Hawk and the Nightingale

A nightingale, sitting aloft upon an oak and singing as usual, was seen by a hawk who, being in need of food, swooped down and seized him. The nightingale, about to lose his life, earnestly begged the hawk to let him go, saying that he was not big enough to satisfy the hunger of a hawk who, if he wanted food, ought to pursue the larger birds. The hawk, interrupting him, said, "I should indeed have lost my senses if I should let go of food ready in my hand for the sake of pursuing birds that are not yet even within sight."

Moral: It is better to take the opportunities you're presented with than to wait for perfection.

The Travelers and the Plane Tree

Two travelers walking in the noonday sun sought the shade of a wide-spreading tree to rest. As they lay looking up among the pleasant leaves, they saw that it was a plane tree. "How useless is the plane!" said one of them. "It bears no fruit whatever, and only serves to litter the ground with leaves."

"Ungrateful creatures!" said a voice from the plane tree. "You lie here in my cooling shade and yet you say I am useless! Thus ungratefully, O Jupiter, do men receive their blessings!"

Moral: Our best blessings are often overlooked.

The Heron

A heron was walking sedately along the bank of a stream, his eyes on the clear water and his long neck and pointed bill ready to snap up a likely morsel for his breakfast. The clear water swarmed with fish, but Master Heron was hard to please that morning. "No small fry for me," he said. "Such scanty fare is not fit for a heron." Now a fine young perch swam near. "No indeed," said the heron. "I wouldn't even trouble to open my beak for anything like that!" As the sun rose, the fish left the shallow water near the shore and swam below into the cool depths toward the middle. The heron saw no more fish and he was very glad at last to breakfast on a tiny snail.

Moral: Someone who is too hard to please may end up with nothing at all.

Part II

Assessing Strong Readers and Writers

We think that the best way to enable students to earn high scores on any kind of test question is to give them practice in every kind of task they'll be asked to perform.

Some questions are basic comprehension questions between the reader and the text, answering "Did you understand what you read?" It's like the relationship between food on a plate and the person eating the food: Can you talk about what you're eating? What's that orange stuff?

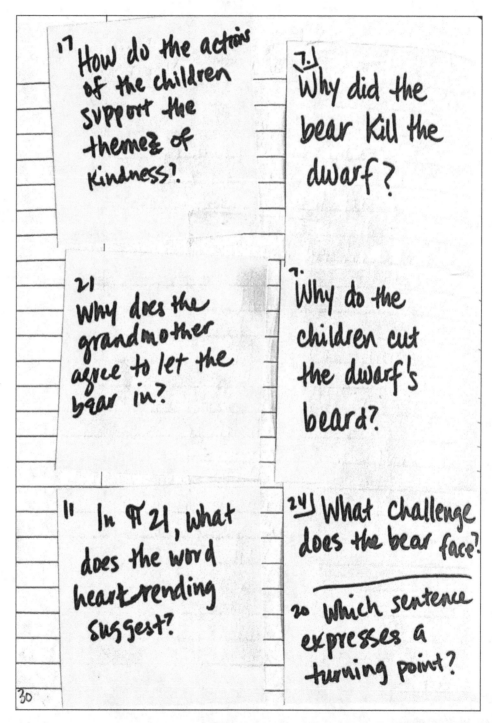

Other questions are triangular, examining the relationship between the reader, the author, and the text: Why did the cook serve up the meal on this kind of plate? What did this chef use to make vegetables seem like meat? What effect did that have on you, the eater?

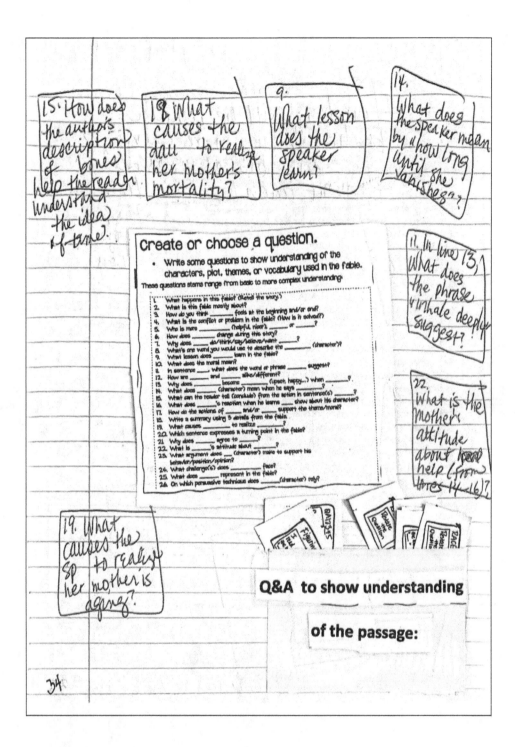

We think the best way to acquaint students with test items is to do the following:

1. Have them read something.

2. Have them write a question.

3. Have them use a structure to guide answering the question.

4. Have them listen to multiple answers from others.

We like to color code tasks, cut and paste structures and question stems into our journals, and keep copies of texts we like in our journals. Why? Students learn better when they can see what they're working on.

Once a student has written a question and answered it, the writing can be expanded into an essay. How? Mostly by taking each sentence and imagining that a listener is confused, then slowing down and explaining it.

1. What happens in this fable? (Retell the story.)
2. What is this fable mostly about?
3. How do you think _____ feels at the beginning and/or end?
4. What is the conflict or problem in the fable? (How is it solved?)
5. Who is more _____ (helpful, nicer), _____ or _____?
6. How does _____ change during this story?
7. Why does _____ do/think/say/believe/want _____?
8. What's one word you would use to describe the _____ (character)?
9. What lesson does _____ learn in the fable?
10. What does the moral mean?
11. In sentence _____, what does the word or phrase _____ suggest?
12. How are _____ and _____ alike/different?
13. Why does _____ become _____ (upset, happy...) when _____?
14. What does _____ (character) mean when he says _____?
15. What can the reader tell (conclude) from the action in sentence(s) _____?
16. What does _____'s reaction when he learns _____ show about his character?
17. How do the actions of _____ and/or _____ support the theme/moral?
18. Write a summary using 3 details from the fable.
19. What causes _____ to realize _____?
20. Which sentence expresses a turning point in the fable?
21. Why does _____ agree to _____?
22. What is _____'s attitude about _____?
23. What argument does ___ (character) make to support his behavior/position/opinion?
24. What challenge(s) does _____ face?
25. What does _____ represent in the fable?
26. On which persuasive technique does _____ (character) rely?

to show understanding of the

characters, plot, themes, or vocabulary

LESSON 4. WRITING ANSWERS TO COMPREHENSION QUESTIONS

4

For many years, students have been answering multiple-choice reading questions to show their understanding of a text. If you agree with Louise Rosenblatt that reading is an act of composing meaning, then you might also believe that those multiple-choice questions can only give us flawed glimpses of a student's understanding of a text, since that student is having to reason out not their own reactions to the text but the reactions of someone else (someone writing the test questions).

Therefore, if students can answer questions about the meaning of a text by sharing their thinking with constructed responses, then their reasoned interpretations have a much wider chance of successfully demonstrating their understanding.

We need to make sure they know not only how to read but also how to articulate their understanding of specific texts as the meaning is unveiled to them. The questions ask, "What do you know?" and text evidence helps them with answering, "How do you know it?"

Step 1. Read a fable.

Step 2. Use the question stems bank.

Use the bank of question stems to create questions. (If each student writes one question, you'll have a collection of great questions.)

1. What happens in this fable? (Retell the story.)
2. What is this fable mostly about?
3. How do you think _____ feels at the beginning and/or end?
4. What is the conflict or problem in the fable? (How is it solved?)
5. Who is more _____ (helpful, nicer), _____ or _____?
6. How does _____ change during this story?
7. Why does _____ do/think/say/believe/want _____?
8. What's one word you would use to describe _____ (character)?
9. What lesson does _____ learn in the fable?
10. What does the moral mean?
11. In sentence ___, what does the word or phrase _____ suggest?
12. How are _____ and _____ alike/different?
13. Why does _____ become _____ (upset, happy) when _____?
14. What does _____ (character) mean when he says _____?
15. What can the reader tell (conclude) from the action in sentence(s) ___?
16. What does ___'s reaction when he learns ___ show about his character?
17. How do the actions of ___ and/or ___ support the theme/moral?
18. Write a summary using 3 details from the fable.
19. What causes _____ to realize _____?
20. Which sentence expresses a turning point in the fable?
21. Why does _____ agree to _____?
22. What is _____'s attitude about _____?
23. What argument does ___ (character) make to support his behavior/opinion?
24. What challenge(s) does _____ face?
25. What does _____ represent in the fable?
26. On which persuasive technique does _____ (character) rely?

Q & A – About Understanding the Reading

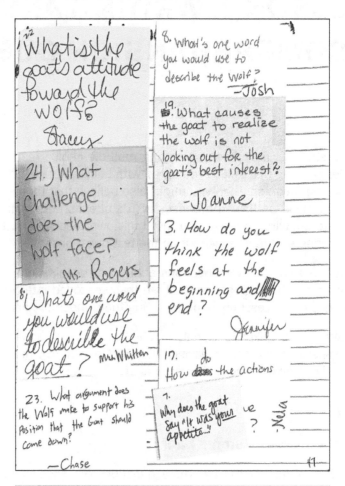

What is the goat's attitude toward the wolf?
Stacey

24.) What challenge does the wolf face?
Ms. Rogers

8. What's one word you would use to describe the goat?
Mrs Whitten

23. What argument does the wolf make to support his position that the goat should come down?
—Chase

8. What's one word you would use to describe the wolf?
—Josh

19. What causes the goat to realize the wolf is not looking out for the goat's best interest?
—Joanne

3. How do you think the wolf feels at the beginning and end?
Jennifer

17. How do the actions

7. Why does the goat say "It was your appetite..."?
—Neda

11

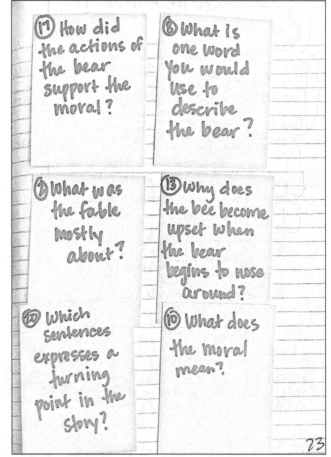

17 How did the actions of the bear support the moral?

8 What is one word you would use to describe the bear?

2 What was the fable mostly about?

13 Why does the bee become upset when the bear begins to nose around?

20 Which sentences expresses a turning point in the story?

10 What does the moral mean?

23

Step 3. Answer the question.

Step 4. Ask yourself, "How do I know this? What did I read that told me this?"

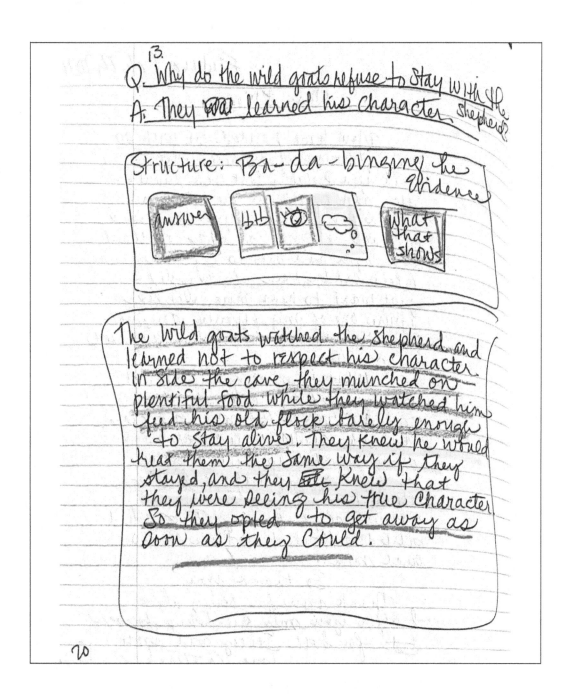

13.
Q. Why do the wild goats refuse to stay with the shepherd?
A. They ~~was~~ learned his character.

Structure: Ba-da-binging the evidence

answer | HtHb 👁 ☁ | What that shows

The wild goats watched the shepherd and learned not to respect his character. Inside the cave, they munched on plentiful food while they watched him feed his old flock barely enough to stay alive. They knew he would treat them the same way if they stayed, and they ~~knew~~ knew that they were seeing his true character. So they opted to get away as soon as they could.

20

Step 5. Choose a text structure.

Find one that will best explain your thinking.

Say or write a sentence for each box from your structure.

You've just created a constructed response!

Step 6. Read your question and response to several people.

UNDERSTANDING WHAT YOU READ: CONSTRUCTED RESPONSE QUESTIONS

1. What happens in this fable? (Retell the story.)

2. What is this fable mostly about?

3. How do you think _____ feels at the beginning and/or end?

4. What is the conflict or problem in the fable? How is it solved?

5. Who is _____ (more helpful, nicer), _____ or _____?

6. How does _____ change during this story?

7. Why does _____ do/think/say/believe/want _____?

8. What's one word you would use to describe _____ (the character)?

9. What lesson does _____ learn in the fable?

10. What does the moral mean?

11. In sentence ___, what does the word or phrase _____ suggest?

12. How are _____ and _____ alike/different?

13. Why does _____ become _____ (upset, happy) when _____?

14. What does _____ mean when they say _____?

15. What can the reader tell (conclude) from the action in sentence(s) _____?

16. What does _____'s reaction when they learn _____ show about their character?

17. How do the actions of ____ and/or ____ support the theme/moral?

18. Write a summary using three details from the fable.

19. What causes _____ to realize _____?

20. Which sentence expresses a turning point in the fable?

21. Why does _____ agree to _____?

22. What is _____'s attitude about _____?

23. What argument does _____ make to support their behavior/position/opinion?

24. What challenge(s) does _____ face?

25. What does _____ represent in the fable?

26. On which persuasive technique does _____ rely?

Structures for Answering Questions About a Text

QA12345

| Question | Answer | How do you know? | What does that mean? | How else do you know | So ... your answer is? |

RACE

| Restate the question | Answer | Cite evidence from the text | Explain what the evidence means |

Ba-da-binging the Evidence

| Answer to the question | How I know  what the character did, saw, thought | What that shows |

Figuring Out the Reading

| I read the words "_____" | Which told me _____ | Then I read "_____" | Which told me _____ | And then I knew _____ |

Explaining a Change

| How _____ changes in the story | At the beginning (with evidence) | At the end (with evidence) | Another way to describe the change |

STUDENT SAMPLES

RACE: "The Lion and the Mouse"
Alex Roldan, Grade 2

Q: Who is more helpful, the lion or the mouse?

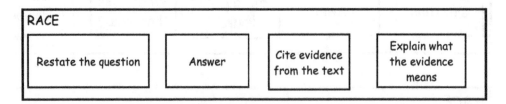

1. Who is more helpful, the lion or the mouse?
2. The lion is more helpful.
3. The text says he was generous and finally let the mouse go.
4. The lion let him live.

Explaining a Change: "The Dog and the Reflection"
Colton Inglish, Grade 6

Q: How do you think the dog feels at the beginning and end of the story?

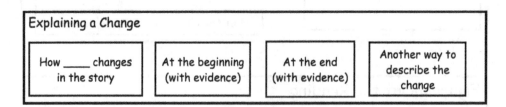

At the beginning of the story, the dog feels happy and perhaps even lucky to have acquired the piece of meat. At the end, he feels sour due to being overcome by greed. I know this because if he wanted another piece of meat enough to risk his own piece of meat, then the piece of meat is important to him, and that justifies his feelings pre- and post-bridge.

Ba-da-binging the Evidence: "The Donkey and the Wolf"
Pedro Moya, Grade 9

Question: What does the wolf learn in the fable?

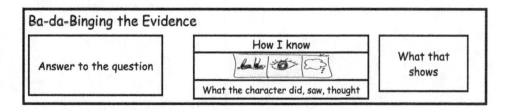

The wolf learned that he should stick with what he knows best, which is hunting, not being a doctor.

The wolf came up to the donkey to remove the thorn. The wolf decided to look for the thorn and the donkey kicked the wolf. Then the wolf says, "Serves me right."

This shows that the wolf learned that he should stick to what he knows best—butchering.

RACE: *Love That Dog*
Lily Thurston, Grade 4

Q: What lesson did Jack learn from Miss Stretchberry?

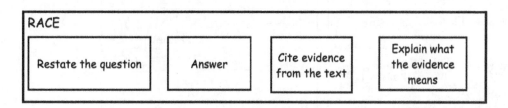

What lesson did Jack learn from Miss Stretchberry? Jack learned that boys can write poems, too. I know because at the start he said, "I don't want to because boys don't write poetry. Girls do." But in the end he wrote a really good poem and got inspired by Mr. Walter Dean Myers, and he learned that not only girls can write poetry.

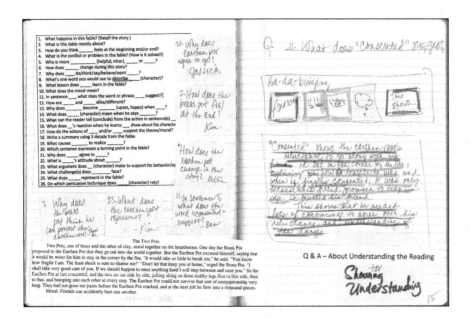

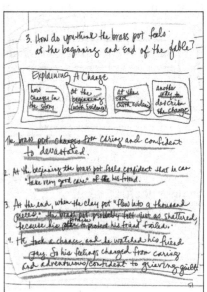

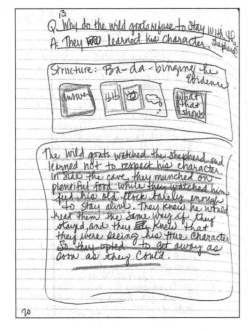

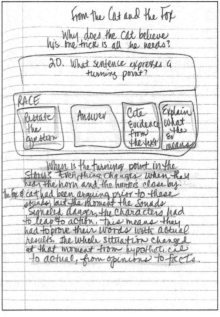

Apply this process to other types of text, such as this letter from John Steinbeck to his son or these two fairy tales:

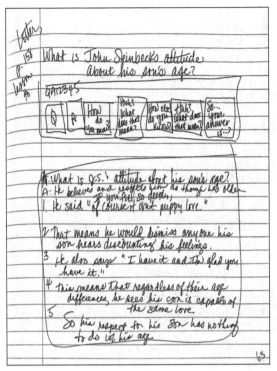

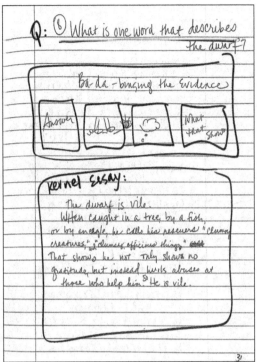

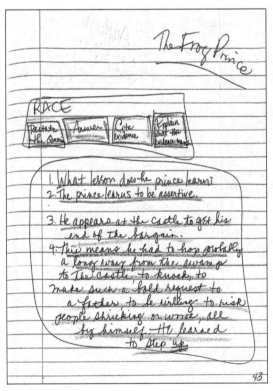

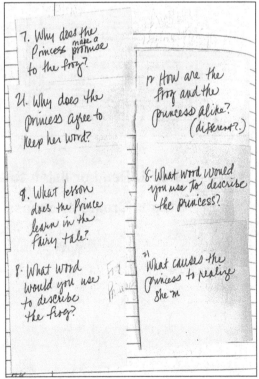

5

LESSON 5. WRITING ANSWERS ABOUT THE AUTHOR'S CRAFT

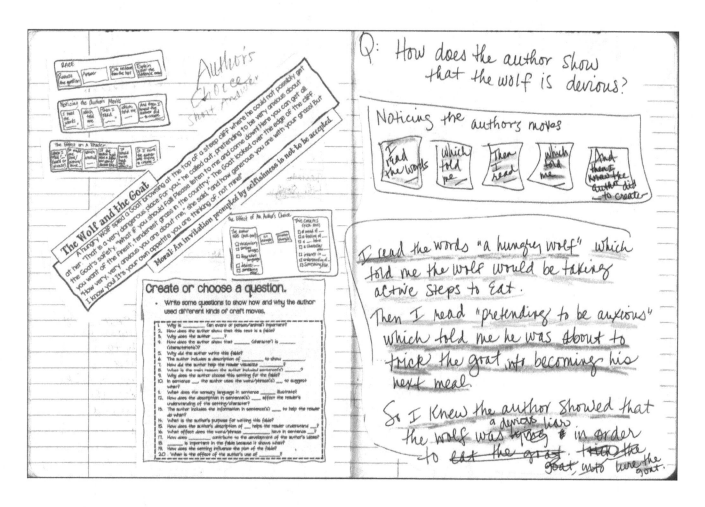

Step 1. Read or listen to a fable.

Step 2. Create or choose a question.

1. Why is _____ (an event or person/animal) important?
2. How does the author show that this text is a fable?
3. Why does the author _____?
4. How does the author show that _____ (character) is _____ (characteristic)?
5. Why did the author write this fable?
6. The author includes a description of _____ to show _____.
7. How did the author help the reader visualize _____?
8. What is the main reason the author included sentence(s) _____?
9. Why does the author choose this setting for the fable?
10. In sentence ___, the author uses the word/phrase(s) ___ to suggest what?
11. What does the sensory language in sentence _____ illustrate?
12. How does the description in sentence(s) ___ affect the reader's understanding of the setting/character?
13. The author includes the information in sentence(s) ___ to help the reader do what?
14. What is the author's purpose for writing this fable?
15. How does the author's description of ___ helps the reader understand ___?
16. What effect does the word/phrase _____ have in sentence ___?
17. How does _____ contribute to the development of the author's ideas?
18. _____ is important in the fable because it shows what?
19. How does the setting influence the plot of the fable?
20. What is the effect of the author's use of _____?

Noticing the A...

figurative language device: _____; I read the words " ", which told me _____; something else.

Structures for Answering Questions

about Author's Choices

Step 3. Answer the question.

Step 4. Ask yourself, "How do I know this?"

What did you read that told you this?

Step 5. Choose a text structure.

Step 6. Write a little for each box.

Step 7. Share.

AUTHOR'S CHOICE QUESTIONS FROM SIMPLER TO MORE COMPLEX

1. Why is _____ (an event or person/animal) important in the fable?

2. How does the author show that this text is a fable?

3. Why does the author ___?

4. How can you tell that _____ (character) is _____ (characteristic)?

5. Why did the author write this fable?

6. The author includes a description of _____ to show _____.

7. How did the author help the reader visualize _____?

8. What is the main reason the author included sentence(s) _____?

9. Why does the author choose this setting for the fable?

10. In sentence ___, the author uses the phrase(s) _____ to suggest what?

11. What does the sensory language in sentence _____ illustrate?

12. How does the description in sentence(s) ___ affect the reader's understanding of the setting?

13. The author includes the information in sentence(s) ___ to help the reader do what?

14. What is the author's purpose for writing this fable?

15. How does the author's description of _____ help the reader understand _____?

16. What effect does the word _____ have in sentence ___?

17. How does _____ contribute to the development of the author's ideas?

18. _____ is important in the fable because it shows what?

19. How does the setting influence the plot of the fable?

20. What is the effect of the author's use of _____?

21. Why is it important in the story that _____ (does/goes to/says) _____?

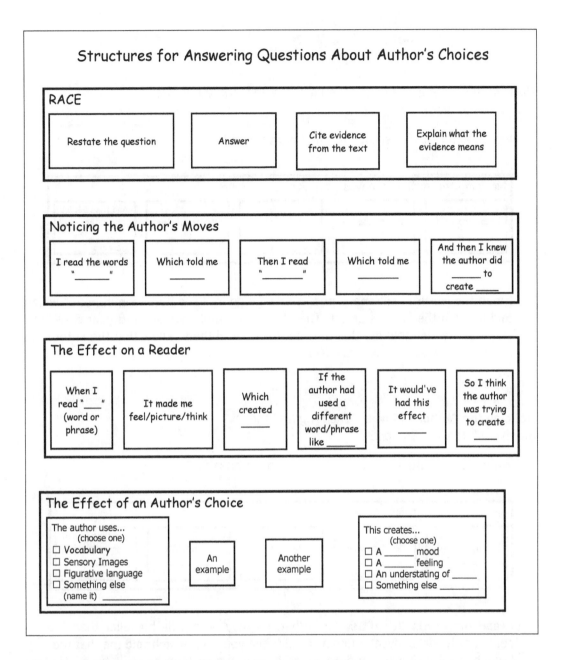

Structures for Answering Questions About Author's Choices

RACE

| Restate the question | Answer | Cite evidence from the text | Explain what the evidence means |

Noticing the Author's Moves

| I read the words "_____" | Which told me _____ | Then I read "_____" | Which told me _____ | And then I knew the author did _____ to create _____ |

The Effect on a Reader

| When I read "___" (word or phrase) | It made me feel/picture/think | Which created _____ | If the author had used a different word/phrase like _____ | It would've had this effect _____ | So I think the author was trying to create _____ |

The Effect of an Author's Choice

The author uses...
(choose one)
☐ Vocabulary
☐ Sensory Images
☐ Figurative language
☐ Something else (name it) _____

An example

Another example

This creates...
(choose one)
☐ A _____ mood
☐ A _____ feeling
☐ An understating of _____
☐ Something else _____

Tips: Adding details to this short writing can transform your short answers into a literary analysis essay.

Also, middle school teacher Michael Brinkley commented, "Once they have written this, we can layer on mini lessons" to revise the response in any of the following ways:

- Naming the title, author, and genre in the opening

- Using the literary present tense

- Choosing a few vague or ordinary words to sharpen the specificity (with a thesaurus)

- Eliminating repeated words

- Replacing "to be" verbs with stronger action verbs

As Brinkley said, "The structure provides the important content, like the food on the plate; now we can show them how to dress it up, like the presentation."

STUDENT SAMPLES

Noticing the Author's Moves: "The Lion, the Fox, and the Beasts"
Zoran Sykes, Grade 2

Q: How does the author show that the fox was wise?

I read the words "I see many hoof-marks going in, I see none coming out," **which told me** that the fox was smart. **Then I read** "All that have entered your cave have stayed in," **which told me** that they got eaten. **And then I knew that the author** did this to show that the fox was wise.

Noticing the Author's Moves: "The Frog and the Ox"
Stephen Matthews, Grade 12

Q. How does the author show that the old frog is boastful?

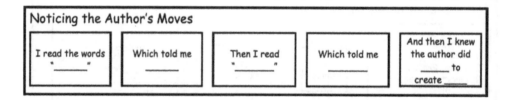

I read the words "It isn't so big either; he may be a little bit taller than I, but I could easily make myself quite as broad; just you see," **which told me** that the frog thought a lot of himself and imagined he was bigger than he really was. (He had told himself lies that were going to cost him a lot later on.) **Then I read**, "So the frog took a deep breath and blew and blew and blew and swelled and swelled and swelled . . . but at this moment, he burst," **which told me** that the desire to make himself look bigger, his pride, and his desire to receive approval from others hurt him because he had already decided he would do anything to receive approval from others. **And then I knew the author** used repetition and clues in the frog's words and actions to show us just where boastfulness would lead.

RACE: "The Frog and the Ox"
Layla Chin, Grade 4

The Effect of an Author's Choice

The author uses... (choose one)	An example	Another example	This creates... (choose one)
☐ Vocabulary ☐ Sensory Images ☐ Figurative language ☐ Something else (name it) _____			☐ A _____ mood ☐ A _____ feeling ☐ An understating of _____ ☐ Something else _____

Q: The moral is important because it shows what?

A: The moral is important to the story because it give the reader understanding of the point of the story. At the end of the story, the frog said, "I'm sure the ox is not as big as—." The frog was just bringing trouble to himself because when he was showing off, he blew up. His own bragging led to his destruction. The moral said it in another way.

GLIMPSES FROM JOURNALS

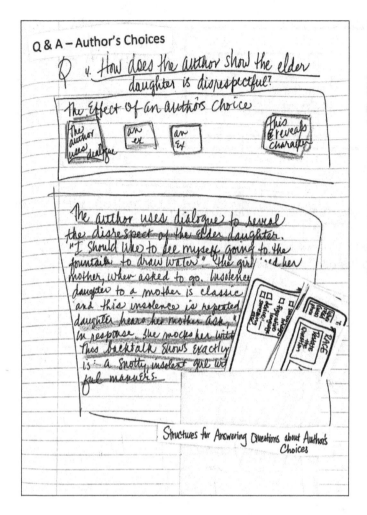

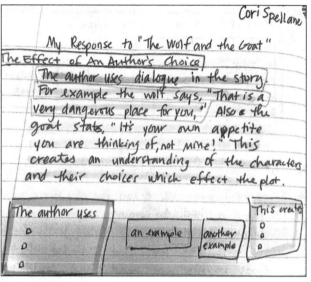

Extensions: Keep these question stems and answer structures in a writer's notebook to use for questions about texts of any genre.

Create or choose a question.

- Write some questions to show how and why the author used different kinds of craft moves.

1. Why is _____ (an event or person/animal) important?
2. How does the author show that this text is a fable?
3. Why does the author _____?
4. How does the author show that _____ (character) is _____ (characteristic)?
5. Why did the author write this fable?
6. The author includes a description of _____ to show _____.
7. How did the author help the reader visualize _____?
8. What is the main reason the author included sentence(s) _____?
9. Why does the author choose this setting for the fable?
10. In sentence ___, the author uses the word/phrase(s) ___ to suggest what?
11. What does the sensory language in sentence _____ illustrate?
12. How does the description in sentence(s) ___ affect the reader's understanding of the setting/character?
13. The author includes the information in sentence(s) ___ to help the reader do what?
14. What is the author's purpose for writing this fable?
15. How does the author's description of ___ helps the reader understand ___?
16. What effect does the word/phrase _____ have in sentence ___?
17. How does _____ contribute to the development of the author's ideas?
18. _____ is important in the fable because it shows what?
19. How does the setting influence the plot of the fable?
20. What is the effect of the author's use of _____?

Q&A about Author's Choices

RACE

| Restate the question | Answer | Cite evidence from the text | Explain what the evidence mean |

Noticing the Authors Moves

| I read the words ___ | Which told me ___ | Then I read ___ | which told me ___ | And then I knew the author did ___ to create ___ |

The Effect on A Reader

| When I read "___" (word or phrase) | It made me feel/ picture/ think ___ | which created ___ | If the author had used a differ -ent word/ phrase like ___ | It would have had this effect ___ | So I think the author was trying to create ___ |

The Effect of An Author's Choice

The author uses (pick one)
☐ vocabulary
☐ sensory images
☐ figurative language
☐ device: ___
☐ something else

an example   another example

This creates (pick me)
☐ a mood of ___
☐ a feeling of ___
☐ a ___ tone
☐ a character who ___
☐ interest in ___
☐ understanding of ___
☐ something else

36

Here, they are used to analyze the poems "My Mother's Tortilla" by Joanne Diaz and "At the Lake" as well as the fairy tale "Diamonds and Toads."

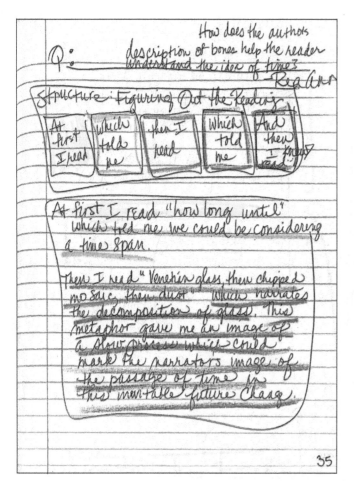

Q: How does the authors description of bones help the reader understand the idea of time?

Structure: Figuring Out the Reading

At first I read | Which told me | then I read | Which told me | And then I know

At first I read "how long until" which told me we could be considering a time span.

Then I read "Venetian glass, then chipped mosaic, then dust" which narrates the decomposition of glass. This metaphor gave me an image of a slow process which could mark the narrators image of the passage of time in this inevitable future change.

35

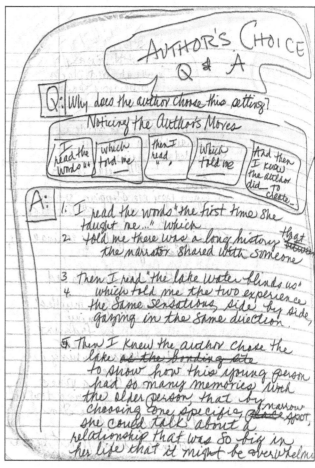

AUTHOR'S CHOICE
Q & A

Q: Why does the author choose this setting?

Noticing the Authors Moves

I read the words "" | which told me | then I read "," | Which told me | And then I knew the author did _ To _ create _

A:
1. I read the words "the first time she taught me..." Which
2. told me there was a long history that the narrator shared with someone
3. Then I read "the lake water blinds us"
4. which told me the two experience the same sensations, side by side, gazing in the same direction.
5. Then I knew the author chose the lake as the bonding site to show how this young person had so many memories with the older person, that by narrow choosing one specific place spot, she could talk about a relationship that was so big in her life that it might be overwhelm

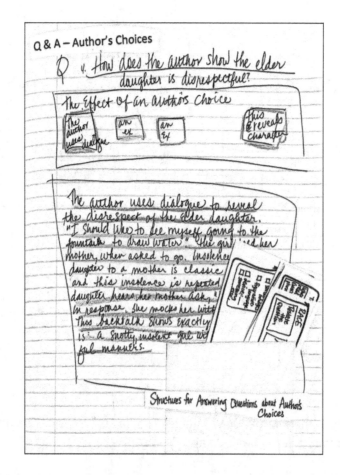

Q & A – Author's Choices

Q4. How does the author show the elder daughter is disrespectful?

The Effect of an Author's Choice

The author uses dialogue | an ex | an Ex | This reveals character

The author uses dialogue to reveal the disrespect of the elder daughter. "I should like to see myself going to the fountain to draw water," the girl ...ed her mother, when asked to go. Insolence daughter to a mother is classic and this insolence is repeated daughter hears her mother ask, ... in response, she mocks her with This backtalk shows exactly ... is a snotty, insolent girl wi... ful manners.

Structures for Answering Questions about Authors Choices

The Birds, the Beasts, and the Bat

The birds and the beasts declared war against each other. No compromise was possible, and so they went at it tooth and claw. It is said the quarrel grew out of the persecution that the race of geese suffered at the teeth of the fox family. The beasts, too, had cause for fight. The eagle was constantly pouncing on the hare, and the owl dined daily on mice. It was a terrible battle. Many a hare and many a mouse died. Chickens and geese fell by the score—and the victor always stopped for a feast. Now, the bat family had not openly joined either side. They were a politic and fickle lot. So when they saw the birds getting the better of it, they were birds for all there was in it. But when the tide of battle turned, they immediately sided with the beasts. When the battle was over, the conduct of the bats was discussed at the peace conference. Such unfaithfulness was unpardonable, and birds and beasts had common cause to drive out the bats. And since then, the bat family hides in dark towers and deserted ruins, flying out only in the night.

Moral: The fickle have no friends.

The Donkey and the Wolf

A donkey was feeding in a pasture near a wood when he saw a wolf lurking in the shadows along the hedge. He easily guessed what the wolf had in mind and thought of a plan to save himself. He pretended he was lame and began to hobble painfully. When the wolf came up, he asked the donkey what had made him lame, and the donkey replied that he had stepped on a sharp thorn. "Please pull it out," he pleaded, groaning as if in pain. "If you do not, it might stick in your throat when you eat me." The wolf saw the wisdom of the advice, for he wanted to enjoy his meal without any danger of choking. So the donkey lifted up his foot and the wolf began to search very closely and carefully for the thorn. Just then, the donkey kicked out with all his might, tumbling the wolf a dozen paces away. And while the wolf was getting very slowly and painfully to his feet, the donkey galloped away in safety. "Serves me right," growled the wolf as he crept into the bushes. "I'm a butcher by trade, not a doctor."

Moral: It is wise to stick to your trade.

The Dog and the Reflection

A dog was carrying a piece of meat in his mouth to eat it in peace at home. On his way, he had to cross a bridge across a brook. As he crossed, he looked down and saw his own reflection in the water. Thinking it was another dog with another piece of meat, he made up his mind to have that also. He made a snap at the shadow in the water, but as he opened his mouth, the piece of meat fell out, dropped into the water, and was lost.

Moral: It is foolish to be greedy.

The Miller, His Son, and Their Donkey

One day, a long time ago, an old miller and his son were on their way to market with a donkey, which they hoped to sell. They drove him very slowly, for they thought they would have a better chance to sell him if they kept him in good condition. As they walked along the highway, some travelers laughed loudly at them. "What foolishness," cried one, "to walk when they might as well ride. The most stupid of the three is not the one you would expect it to be." The miller did not like to be laughed at, so he told his son to climb up and ride.

They had gone a little farther along the road, when three merchants passed by. "Oh, what have we here?" they cried. "Respect old age, young man! Get down and let the old man ride." Though the miller was not tired, he made the boy get down and climbed up himself to ride, just to please the merchants.

At the next turnstile, they overtook some women carrying market baskets loaded with vegetables and other things to sell. "Look at the old fool," exclaimed one of them. "Perched on the donkey, while that poor boy has to walk." The miller felt a bit vexed, but to be agreeable, he told the boy to climb up behind him.

They had no sooner started out again than a loud shout went up from another company of people on the road. "What a crime," cried one, "to load up a poor dumb beast like that! They look more able to carry the poor creature than he to carry them."

"They must be on their way to sell the poor thing's hide," said another. The miller and his son quickly scrambled down, and a short time later, the marketplace was thrown into an uproar as the two came along carrying the donkey slung from a pole. A great crowd of people ran out to get a closer look at the strange sight. The donkey did not dislike being carried, but so many people came up to point at him and laugh and shout that he began to kick and bray and then, just as they were crossing a bridge, the ropes that held him gave way and down he tumbled into the river. The poor miller now set out sadly for home. By trying to please everybody, he had pleased nobody and lost his donkey besides.

Moral: If you try to please all, you please none.

The Seagull and the Owl

A hungry seagull, having bolted down too large a fish, burst its deep gullet-bag and lay down on the shore to die. An owl saw him and exclaimed, "You richly deserve your fate; for a bird of the air has no business to seek its food from the sea!"

Moral: No rule of nature applies to everyone the same way.

The Astrologer

A man who lived a long time ago believed that he could read the future in the stars. He called himself an astrologer and spent his time at night gazing at the sky. One evening, he was walking along the open road outside the village. His eyes were fixed on the stars. He thought he saw there that the end of the world was at hand, when all at once, down he went into a hole full of mud and water. There he stood up to his ears in the muddy water and madly clawed at the slippery sides of the hole in his effort to climb out. His cries for help soon brought the villagers running. As they pulled him out of the mud, one of them said: "You pretend to read the future in the stars, and yet you fail to see what is at your feet! This may teach you to pay more attention to what is right in front of you and let the future take care of itself."

"What use is it," said another, "to read the stars, when you can't see what's right here on the earth?"

Moral: If you take care of the little things, the big things will take care of themselves.

The Bees, the Wasps, and the Hornet

A store of honey had been found in a hollow tree, and the wasps declared positively that it belonged to them. The bees were just as sure that the treasure was theirs. The argument grew very pointed, and it looked as if the affair could not be settled without a battle when at last, with much good sense, they agreed to let a judge decide the matter. So they brought the case before the hornet, who was the justice of the peace in that part of the woods. When the judge called the case, witnesses declared that they had seen certain winged creatures in the neighborhood of the hollow tree, who hummed loudly and whose bodies were striped yellow and black like bees. Counsel for the wasps immediately insisted that this description fitted his clients exactly. Such evidence did not help Judge Hornet to any decision, so he adjourned court for six weeks to give him time to think it over. When the case came up again, both sides had a large number of witnesses. An ant was first to take the stand, and was about to be cross-examined, when a wise old bee addressed the court. "Your honor," he said, "the case has now been pending for six weeks. If it is not decided soon, the honey will not be fit for anything. I move that the bees and the wasps be both instructed to build a honeycomb. Then we shall soon see to whom the honey really belongs." The wasps protested loudly. Wise Judge Hornet quickly understood why they did so: They knew they could not build a honeycomb and fill it with honey.

"It is clear," said the judge, "who made the comb and who could not have made it. The honey belongs to the bees."

Moral: A wise man can find out the truth.

The Cat and the Fox

Once a cat and a fox were traveling together. As they went along, picking up provisions on the way—a stray mouse here, a fat chicken there—they began an argument to while away the time between bites. And, as usually happens when comrades argue, the talk began to get personal. "You think you are extremely clever, don't you?" said the fox. "Do you pretend to know more than I? Why, I know a whole sack full of tricks!"

"Well," retorted the cat, "I admit I know one trick only, but that one, let me tell you, is worth a thousand of yours!" Just then, close by, they heard a hunter's horn and the yelping of a pack of hounds. In an instant, the cat was up a tree, hiding among the leaves. "This is my trick," he called to the fox. "Now let me see what yours are worth." But the fox had so many plans for escape that he could not decide which one to try first. He dodged here and there with the hounds at his heels. He doubled on his tracks, he ran at top speed, he entered a dozen burrows—but all in vain. The hounds caught him and soon put an end to the boaster and all his tricks.

Moral: Sometimes fewer choices are better.

The Wild Boar and the Fox

A wild boar was sharpening his tusks busily against the stump of a tree when a fox happened by. Now, the fox was always looking for a chance to make fun of his neighbors. So he made a great show of looking anxiously about, as if in fear of some hidden enemy. But the boar kept right on with his work. "Why are you doing that?" asked the fox at last with a grin. "There isn't any danger that I can see."

"True enough," replied the boar, "but when danger does come, there will not be time for such work as this. My weapons will have to be ready for use then or I shall suffer for it."

Moral: Preparedness for war can guarantee peace.

The Young Man and the Swallow

A young fellow who was very popular among his companions as a good spender quickly wasted his fortune trying to live up to his reputation. One fine day in early spring, he found himself with not a penny left and no property, save the clothes he wore. He was to meet some jolly young men that morning, and he was at his wits' end figuring out how to get enough money to keep up appearances. Just then, a swallow flew by, twittering merrily, and the young man, thinking summer had come, hastened off to a clothes dealer to whom he sold all the clothes he wore, down to his very tunic. A few days later, a change in weather brought a severe frost. The poor swallow and that foolish young man in his light tunic, with his arms and knees bare, could scarcely keep life in their shivering bodies.

Moral: One swallow does not make a summer.

The Lark and Her Young Ones

A lark made her nest in a field of young wheat. As the days passed, the wheat stalks grew tall and the young birds, too, grew in strength. Then one day, when the ripe golden grain waved in the breeze, the farmer and his son came into the field. "This wheat is now ready for reaping," said the farmer. "We must call in our neighbors and friends to help us harvest it."

The young larks in their nest close by were much frightened, for they knew they would be in great danger if they did not leave the nest before the reapers came. When the mother lark returned with food for them, they told her what they had heard. "Do not be frightened, children," said the mother lark. "If the farmer said he would call in his neighbors and friends to help him do his work, this wheat will not be reaped for a while yet."

A few days later, the wheat was so ripe that when the wind shook the stalks, a hail of wheat grains came rustling down on the young larks' heads. "If this wheat is not harvested at once," said the farmer, "we shall lose half the crop. We cannot wait any longer for help from our friends. Tomorrow we must set to work ourselves."

When the young larks told their mother what they had heard that day, she said, "Then we must be off at once. When a man decides to do his own work and not depend on anyone else, then you may be sure there will be no more delay." There was much fluttering and trying out of wings that afternoon, and at sunrise the next day, when the farmer and his son cut down the grain, they found an empty nest.

Moral: Self-help is the best help.

Belling the Cat

The mice once called a meeting to decide on a plan to free themselves of their enemy, the cat. At least they wished to find some way of knowing when she was coming, so they might have time to run away. Indeed, something had to be done, for they lived in such constant fear of her claws that they hardly dared stir from their dens by night or day. Many plans were discussed, but none of them was thought good enough. At last, a very young mouse got up and said, "I have a plan that seems very simple, but I know it will be successful. All we have to do is to hang a bell about the cat's neck. When we hear the bell ringing, we will know immediately that our enemy is coming."

All the mice were much surprised that they had not thought of such a plan before. But in the midst of the rejoicing over their good fortune, an old mouse arose and said, "I will say that the plan of the young mouse is very good. But let me ask one question: Who will bell the cat?"

Moral: It is easy to say that something should be done; it's difficult to do it.

The Frogs and the Well

Two frogs dwelt in the same pool. When the pool dried up under the summer's heat, they left it and set out together for another home. As they went along, they chanced to pass a deep well, amply supplied with water. When they saw it, one of the frogs said to the other, "Let us descend and make our abode in this well. It will furnish us with shelter and food."

The other replied with greater caution, "But suppose the water should fail us. How can we get out again from so great a depth?'

Moral: The first solution is not always the best one.

The Fox and the Goat

A fox fell into a well, and though it was not very deep, he found that he could not get out again. After he had been in the well a long time, a thirsty goat came by. The goat thought the fox had gone down to drink, and so he asked if the water was good. "The finest in the whole country," said the crafty fox. "Jump in and try it. There is more than enough for both of us." The thirsty goat immediately jumped in and began to drink. The fox just as quickly jumped on the goat's back and leaped from the tip of the goat's horns out of the well. The foolish goat now saw what a plight he had got into and begged the fox to help him out. But the fox was already on his way to the woods. "If you had as much sense as you have beard, old fellow," he said as he ran, "you would have been more cautious about finding a way to get out again before you jumped in."

Moral: It's easy to mock someone for making the same mistake you have made.

The Donkey and the Grasshopper

One day as a donkey was walking in the pasture, he found some grasshoppers chirping merrily in a grassy corner of the field. He listened with a great deal of admiration to the song of the grasshoppers. It was such a joyful song that his pleasure-loving heart was filled with a wish to sing as they did. "What is it," he asked very respectfully, "that has given you such beautiful voices? Is there any special food you eat or is it some divine nectar that makes you sing so wonderfully?"

"Yes," said the grasshoppers, who were very fond of a joke. "It is the dew we drink! Try some and see." So thereafter, the donkey would eat nothing and drink nothing but dew. Naturally, the poor foolish donkey soon died.

Moral: Other people's advice should be tempered with your own common sense.

The Fox Without His Tail

A fox that had been caught in a trap succeeded at last, after much painful tugging, in getting away. But he had to leave his beautiful bushy tail behind him. For a long time, he kept away from the other foxes, for he knew well enough that they would all make fun of him and crack jokes and laugh behind his back. But it was hard for him to live alone, and at last, he thought of a plan that would perhaps help him out of his trouble. He called a meeting of all the foxes, saying that he had something of great importance to tell the tribe. When they were all gathered together, the fox without a tail got up and made a long speech about those foxes who had come to harm because of their tails. This one had been caught by hounds when his tail had become entangled in the hedge. That one had not been able to run fast enough because of the weight of his brush. Besides, it was well known, he said, that men hunt foxes simply for their tails, which they cut off as prizes of the hunt. With such proof of the danger and uselessness of having a tail, said Master Fox, he would advise every fox to cut it off if he valued life and safety. When he had finished talking, an old fox arose and said, smiling, "Master Fox, kindly turn around for a moment, and you shall have your answer." When the poor fox without a tail turned around, there arose such a storm of jeers and hooting that he saw how useless it was to try any longer to persuade the foxes to part with their tails.

Moral: A wise person considers the motive of someone giving advice.

The Ant and the Chrysalis

An ant nimbly running about in the sunshine in search of food came across a chrysalis that was very near its time of changing. The chrysalis moved its tail and thus attracted the attention of the ant, who then saw for the first time that it was alive. "Poor, pitiable animal!" cried the ant disdainfully. "What a sad fate is yours! While I can run hither and thither at my pleasure and, if I wish, ascend the tallest tree, you lie imprisoned here in your shell with power only to move a joint or two of your scaly tail."

The chrysalis heard all this but did not try to make any reply. A few days after, when the ant passed that way again, nothing but the shell remained. Wondering what had become of its contents, he felt himself suddenly shaded and fanned by the gorgeous wings of a beautiful butterfly. "Behold your much-pitied friend!" said the butterfly, "Boast now of your powers to run and climb as long as you can get me to listen." So saying, the butterfly rose in the air and, borne along and aloft on the summer breeze, was soon lost to the sight of the ant forever.

Moral: Pity is often misplaced.

The Fox, the Rooster, and the Dog

A dog and a rooster, who were the best of friends, wished very much to see something of the world. So they decided to leave the farmyard and set out into the world along the road that led to the woods. The two comrades traveled along in the very best of spirits and did not meet any adventure to speak of. At nightfall, the rooster (looking for a place to roost, as was his custom) spied a hollow tree nearby that he thought would do very nicely for a night's lodging. The dog could creep inside and the rooster would fly up on one of the branches. So said, so done, and both slept very comfortably. With the first glimmer of dawn, the rooster awoke. For the moment, he forgot where he was. He thought he was still in the farmyard, where it had been his duty to arouse the household at daybreak. Standing on tiptoe, he flapped his wings and crowed lustily. But instead of awakening the farmer, he awakened a fox not far off in the wood. The fox immediately had rosy visions of a very delicious breakfast. Hurrying to the tree where the rooster was roosting, he said very politely, "A hearty welcome to our woods, honored sir. I cannot tell you how glad I am to see you here. I am quite sure we shall become the closest of friends."

"I feel highly flattered, kind sir," replied the rooster slyly. "If you will please go around to the door of my house at the foot of the tree, my porter will let you in." The hungry but unsuspecting fox went around the tree as he was told, and in a twinkling, the dog had seized him.

Moral: Those who try to deceive may expect to be paid in their own coin.

The Wolf and the Goat

A hungry wolf spied a goat browsing at the top of a steep cliff where he could not possibly get at her. "That is a very dangerous place for you," he called out, pretending to be very anxious about the goat's safety. "What if you should fall? Please listen to me and come down! Here you can get all you want of the finest, tenderest grass in the country."

The goat looked over the edge of the cliff. "How very, very anxious you are about me," she said, "and how generous you are with your grass! But I know you! It's your own appetite you are thinking of, not mine!"

Moral: An invitation prompted by selfishness is not to be accepted.

The Lamb and the Wolf

A stray lamb stood drinking early one morning on the bank of a woodland stream. That very same morning, a hungry wolf came by further up the stream, hunting for something to eat. He soon got his eyes on the lamb. As a rule, Mr. Wolf snapped up such delicious morsels without making any bones about it, but this lamb looked so very helpless and innocent that the wolf felt he ought to have some kind of an excuse for taking its life. "How dare you paddle around in my stream and stir up all the mud!" he shouted fiercely. "You deserve to be punished severely for your rashness!"

"But, your highness," replied the trembling lamb, "do not be angry! I cannot possibly muddy the water you are drinking up there. Remember, you are upstream and I am downstream."

"You do muddy it!" retorted the wolf savagely. "And besides, I have heard that you told lies about me last year!"

"How could I have done so?" pleaded the lamb. "I wasn't born until this year."

"If it wasn't you, it was your brother!"

"I have no brothers."

"Well, then," snarled the wolf, "it was someone in your family anyway. But no matter who it was, I do not intend to be talked out of my breakfast." And without more words, the wolf seized the poor lamb and carried her off to the forest.

Moral: The tyrant can always find an excuse for his tyranny.

The Lion and the Wolf

A wolf, roaming by the mountain's side as the sun was setting, saw his own shadow become greatly extended and magnified, and he said to himself, "Why should I, being of such an immense size, and extending nearly an acre in length, be afraid of the lion? Ought I not to be acknowledged as king of all the collected beasts?" While he was indulging in these proud thoughts, a lion fell upon him and killed him. He exclaimed with a too-late repentance, "Wretched me! This overestimation of myself is the cause of my destruction."

Moral: It is not wise to hold too exalted an opinion of oneself.

The Fox and the Crow

A crow, having stolen a bit of meat, perched in a tree and held it in her beak. A fox, seeing her, longed to possess himself of the meat and, by a wily stratagem, succeeded. "How handsome is the crow," he exclaimed, "in the beauty of her shape and in the fairness of her complexion! Oh, if her voice were only equal to her beauty, she would deservedly be considered the Queen of Birds!" This he said deceitfully, having greater admiration for the meat than for the crow. But the crow, all her vanity aroused by the cunning flattery and anxious to refute the reflection cast upon her voice, set up a loud caw and dropped the meat. The fox quickly picked it up and thus addressed the crow: "My good crow, your voice is right enough, but your wit is wanting."

Moral: He who listens to flattery is not wise, for it has no good purpose.

The Quack Frog

An old frog once informed all his neighbors that he was a learned doctor. In fact, he could cure anything. The fox heard the news and hurried to see the frog. He looked the frog over very carefully. "Mr. Frog," he said, "I've been told that you cure anything! But just take a look at yourself, and then try some of your own medicine. If you can cure yourself of that blotchy skin and that rheumatic gait, someone might believe you. Otherwise, I should advise you to try some other profession."

Moral: Those who would mend others, should first mend themselves.

The Vain Jackdaw

Jupiter determined, it is said, to create a sovereign over the birds and made proclamation that on a certain day they should all present themselves before him, when he would himself choose the most beautiful among them to be king. The jackdaw, knowing his own ugliness, searched through the woods and fields and collected the feathers that had fallen from the wings of his companions and stuck them in all parts of his body. When the appointed day arrived, and the birds had assembled before Jupiter, the jackdaw also made his appearance in his many-feathered finery. Jupiter proposed to make him king on account of the beauty of his plumage, but the birds indignantly protested and each plucked from him his own feathers; the Jackdaw was again nothing but a jackdaw.

Moral: Hope not to succeed in borrowed plumes.

The Fighting Roosters and the Eagle

Two roosters fought for the sovereignty of the dunghill. One was severely beaten and ran and hid himself in a hole. The conqueror flew to the top of an outhouse, flapped his wings, and crowed out, "Victory!" Just then an eagle dived, trussed him, and carried him off. The other, seeing this from his hiding place, came out and, shaking off the recollection of his late disgrace, strutted about among his hens with all the dignity imaginable.

Moral: Pride goes before destruction.

The Wolf and the Lion

A wolf had stolen a lamb and was carrying it off to his lair to eat it. But his plans were very much changed when he met a lion, who, without making any excuses, took the lamb away from him. The wolf made off to a safe distance and said in a much-injured tone, "You have no right to take my property like that!"

The lion looked back, but as the wolf was too far away to be taught a lesson without too much inconvenience, he said, "*Your* property? Did you buy it, or did the shepherd make you a gift of it? Pray tell me, how did you get it?"

Moral: What is won by force can be lost by force.

The Sheep and the Pig

One day, a shepherd discovered a fat pig in the meadow where his sheep were pastured. He very quickly captured the porker, which squealed at the top of its voice the moment the shepherd laid his hands on it. You would have thought, to hear the loud squealing, that the pig was being cruelly hurt. But in spite of its squeals and struggles to escape, the shepherd tucked his prize under his arm and started off to the butcher's in the marketplace. The sheep in the pasture were much astonished and amused at the pig's behavior and followed the shepherd and his charge to the pasture gate. "What makes you squeal like that?" asked one of the sheep. "The shepherd often catches and carries off one of us. But we should feel very much ashamed to make such a terrible fuss about it like you do."

"That is all very well," replied the pig, with a squeal and a frantic kick. "When he catches you, he is only after your wool. But he wants my bacon! Gree-ee-ee!"

Moral: It is easy to be brave when there is no danger.

The Heifer and the Ox

A heifer saw an ox hard at work harnessed to a plow and tormented him with reflections on his unhappy fate in being compelled to labor. Shortly afterwards, at the harvest festival, the owner released the ox from his yoke but bound the heifer with cords and led her away to the altar to be slain in honor of the occasion. The ox saw what was being done and said with a smile to the heifer, "For this you were allowed to live in idleness, because you were presently to be sacrificed."

Moral: It's never right to make fun of others.

The Dove and the Crows

A dove shut up in a cage was boasting of the large number of young ones that she had hatched. A crow, hearing her, said, "My good friend, cease from this unseasonable boasting. The larger the number of your family, the greater your cause of sorrow in seeing them in this prison house."

Moral: Every member of a family brings joy and sorrow.

The Frog and the Ox

"Oh, father," said a little frog to the big one sitting by the side of a pool. "I have seen such a terrible monster! It was as big as a mountain, with horns on its head, and a long tail, and it had hoofs divided in two."

"Tush, child, tush," said the old frog. "That was only Farmer White's ox. It isn't so big either; he may be a little bit taller than I, but I could easily make myself quite as broad; just you see." So the father blew and blew and blew. "Was he as big as that?" he asked.

"Oh, much bigger than that," said the young frog. Again, the old one blew himself up and asked the young one if the ox was as big as that. "Bigger, father, bigger," was the reply.

So the frog took a deep breath and blew and blew and blew and swelled and swelled and swelled. And then he said, "I'm sure the ox is not as big as—" But at this moment, he burst.

Moral: Showing off can lead to self-destruction.

The Old Man and the Three Young Men

As an old man was planting a tree, three young men came along and began to make sport of him, saying, "It shows your foolishness to be planting a tree at your age. The tree cannot bear fruit for many years, while you must very soon die. What is the use of your wasting your time in providing pleasure for others to share long after you are dead?"

The old man stopped in his labor and replied, "Others before me provided for my happiness, and it is my duty to provide for those who shall come after me. As for life, who is sure of it for a day? You may all die before me." The old man's words came true; one of the young men went on a voyage at sea and was drowned, another went to war and was shot, and the third fell from a tree and broke his neck.

Moral: We should plan for those who come after us.

The Donkey Carrying Salt

A merchant, driving his donkey homeward from the seashore with a heavy load of salt, came to a river crossed by a shallow ford. They had crossed this river many times before without accident, but this time, the donkey slipped and fell when halfway over. When the merchant at last got him to his feet, much of the salt had melted away. Delighted to find how much lighter his burden had become, the donkey finished the journey very gayly. The next day, the merchant went for another load of salt. On the way home, the donkey, remembering what had happened at the ford, purposely let himself fall into the water and again got rid of most of his burden. The angry merchant immediately turned about and drove the donkey back to the seashore, where he loaded him with two great baskets of sponges. At the ford, the donkey again tumbled over, but when he had scrambled to his feet, his load was ten times heavier than before.

Moral: The same methods will not suit all circumstances.

The Donkey and His Driver

A donkey was being driven along a road leading down the mountain side when he suddenly took it into his silly head to choose his own path. He could see his stall at the foot of the mountain and to him, the quickest way down seemed to be over the edge of the nearest cliff. Just as he was about to leap over, his master caught him by the tail and tried to pull him back, but the stubborn donkey would not yield and pulled with all his might. "Very well," said his master, "go your way, you willful beast, and see where it leads you." With that, he let go, and the foolish donkey tumbled head over heels down the mountain side.

Moral: Those who will not listen to reason are on the road to misfortune.

The Lion and the Gnat

"Away with you, vile insect!" said a lion angrily to a gnat that was buzzing around his head.

But the gnat was not in the least disturbed. "Do you think," he said spitefully to the lion, "that I am afraid of you because they call you king?" The next instant, he flew at the lion and stung him sharply on the nose. Mad with rage, the lion struck fiercely at the gnat but only succeeded in tearing himself with his claws. Again and again the gnat stung the lion, who now was roaring terribly. At last, worn out with rage and covered with wounds that his own teeth and claws had made, the lion gave up the fight. The gnat buzzed away to tell the whole world about his victory but instead, he flew straight into a spider's web. And there, he who had defeated the king of beasts came to a miserable end, the prey of a little spider.

Moral: Sometimes it's wise to fear the smallest of our enemies.

The Bat and the Weasels

A bat blundered into the nest of a weasel, who ran up to catch and eat him. The bat begged for his life, but the weasel would not listen. "You are a mouse," he said, "and I am a sworn enemy of mice. Every mouse I catch, I am going to eat!"

"But I am not a mouse!" cried the bat. "Look at my wings. Can mice fly? Why, I am only a bird! Please let me go!" The weasel had to admit that the bat was not a mouse, so he let him go.

But a few days later, the foolish bat went blindly into the nest of another weasel. This weasel happened to be a bitter enemy of birds, and he soon had the bat under his claws, ready to eat him. "You are a bird," he said, "and I am going to eat you!"

"What?" cried the bat. "I, a bird! Why, all birds have feathers! I am nothing but a mouse. 'Down with all cats' is my motto!" And so the bat escaped with his life a second time.

Moral: Different circumstances require different responses.

The Bear and the Two Travelers

Two men were traveling in company through a forest, when all at once, a huge bear crashed out of the brush near them. One of the men, thinking of his own safety, climbed a tree. The other, unable to fight the savage beast alone, threw himself on the ground and lay still, as if he were dead. He had heard that a bear will not touch a dead body. It must have been true, for the bear snuffed at the man's head awhile and then, seeming to be satisfied that he was dead, walked away. The man in the tree climbed down. "It looked just as if that bear whispered in your ear," he said. "What did he tell you?"

"He said," answered the other, "that it was not at all wise to keep company with a fellow who would desert his friend in a moment of danger."

Moral: Misfortune is the test of true friendship.

The Hare With Many Friends

A hare was very popular with the other beasts who all claimed to be her friends. But one day, she heard the hounds approaching and hoped to escape them by the aid of her many friends. So, she went to the horse and asked him to carry her away from the hounds on his back. But he declined, stating that he had important work to do for his master. He felt sure, he said, that all her other friends would come to her assistance. She then applied to the bull and hoped that he would repel the hounds with his horns. The bull replied, "I am very sorry, but I have an appointment with a lady; but I feel sure that our friend the goat will do what you want." The goat, however, feared that his back might be harmed if he took her upon it. The ram, he felt sure, was the proper friend to apply to.

So she went to the ram and told him the case. The ram replied, "Another time, my dear friend. I do not like to interfere on the present occasion, as hounds have been known to eat sheep as well as hares." The hare then applied, as a last hope, to the calf, who regretted that he was unable to help her, as he did not like to take the responsibility upon himself as so many older persons than himself had declined the task. By this time, the hounds were quite near and the hare took to her heels and luckily escaped.

Moral: Friendship is proven by actions, not words.

The Farmer and the Stork

A stork of a very simple and trusting nature had been asked by a lively party of cranes to visit a field that had been newly planted. But the party ended dismally with all the birds entangled in the meshes of the farmer's net. The stork begged the farmer to spare him. "Please let me go," he pleaded. "I belong to the stork family who you know are honest and birds of good character. Besides, I did not know the cranes were going to steal."

"You may be a very good bird," answered the farmer, "but I caught you with the thieving cranes and you will have to share the same punishment with them."

Moral: You are judged by the company you keep.

The Dog and the Hare

A hound, having startled a hare on the hillside, pursued her for some distance, at one time biting her with his teeth as if he would take her life and at another fawning upon her as if in play with another dog. The hare said to him, "I wish you would act sincerely by me and show yourself in your true colors. If you are a friend, why do you bite me so hard? If an enemy, why do you fawn on me?"

Moral: Real friends should know whether they can trust each other.

The Wolves and the Sheep

A pack of wolves lurked near the sheep pasture. But the dogs kept them all at a respectful distance and the sheep grazed in perfect safety. But now, the wolves thought of a plan to trick the sheep. "Why is there always this hostility between us?" they asked. "If it were not for those dogs who are always stirring up trouble, I am sure we should get along beautifully. Send them away and you will see what good friends we shall become." The sheep were easily fooled. They persuaded the dogs to go away, and that very evening, the wolves had the grandest feast of their lives.

Moral: It's a bad idea to give up friends for foes.

The Monkey and the Dolphin

It happened once upon a time that a certain Greek ship bound for Athens was wrecked off the coast close to Piraeus, the port of Athens. Had it not been for the dolphins, who at that time were very friendly toward mankind and especially toward Athenians, all would have perished. But the dolphins took the shipwrecked people on their backs and swam with them to shore. Now, it was the custom among the Greeks to take their pet monkeys and dogs with them whenever they went on a voyage. So when one of the dolphins saw a monkey struggling in the water, he thought it was a man and made the monkey climb up on his back. Then off he swam with him toward the shore. The monkey sat up, grave and dignified on the dolphin's back. "You are a citizen of illustrious Athens, are you not?" asked the dolphin politely.

"Yes," answered the monkey, proudly. "My family is one of the noblest in the city."

"Indeed," said the dolphin. "Then of course you often visit Piraeus."

"Yes, yes," replied the monkey. "Indeed, I do. I am with him constantly. Piraeus is my very best friend." This answer took the dolphin by surprise and, turning his head, he now saw what it was he was carrying. Without more ado, he dived and left the foolish monkey to take care of himself, while he swam off in search of some human being to save.

Moral: One falsehood leads to another.

The Eagle, the Cat, and the Wild Sow

An eagle made her nest at the top of a lofty oak; a cat, having found a convenient hole, moved into the middle of the trunk; and a wild sow with her young took shelter in a hollow at its foot. The cat cunningly resolved to destroy this chance-made colony. To carry out her design, she climbed to the nest of the eagle, and said, "Destruction is preparing for you and for me, too, unfortunately. The wild sow, whom you see daily digging up the earth, wishes to uproot the oak, so that she may, on its fall, seize our families as food for her young." Having thus frightened the eagle out of her senses, she crept down to the cave of the sow and said, "Your children are in great danger; for as soon as you go out with your litter to find food, the eagle is prepared to pounce upon one of your little pigs." Having instilled these fears into the sow, she went and pretended to hide herself in the hollow of the tree. When night came, she went forth with silent foot and obtained food for herself and her kittens but, feigning to be afraid, she kept a lookout all through the day. Meanwhile, the eagle, full of fear of the sow, sat still on the branches and the sow, terrified by the eagle, did not dare to go out from her cave. And thus they both (along with their families) perished from hunger and afforded ample provision for the cat and her kittens.

Moral: It's dangerous to be paralyzed by fear.

The Wolf in Sheep's Clothing

A certain wolf could not get enough to eat because of the watchfulness of the shepherds. But one night, he found a sheepskin that had been cast aside and forgotten. The next day, dressed in the skin, the wolf strolled into the pasture with the sheep. Soon, a little lamb was following him about and was quickly led away to slaughter. That evening, the wolf entered the fold with the flock. But it happened that the shepherd took a fancy for mutton broth that very evening and, picking up a knife, went to the fold where the first animal in his path happened to be the wolf.

Moral: The evildoer often comes to harm through his own deceit.

The Rooster and the Fox

One bright evening, as the sun was sinking on a glorious world, a wise old rooster flew into a tree to roost. Before he composed himself to rest, he flapped his wings three times and crowed loudly. But just as he was about to put his head under his wing, his beady eyes caught a flash of red and a glimpse of a long, pointed nose, and there just below him stood Master Fox. "Have you heard the wonderful news?" cried the fox in a very joyful and excited manner.

"What news?" asked the rooster very calmly. But he had a fluttery feeling inside him, for he was very much afraid of the fox.

"Your family and mine and all other animals have agreed to forget their differences and live in peace and friendship from now on forever. Just think of it! I simply cannot wait to embrace you! Do come down, dear friend, and let us celebrate the joyful event."

"How grand!" said the rooster. "I certainly am delighted at the news." But he spoke in an absent way and, stretching up on tiptoes, seemed to be looking at something afar off.

"What is it you see?" asked the fox a little anxiously.

"Why, it looks to me like a couple of dogs coming this way. They must have heard the good news and—" But the fox did not wait to hear more. Off he started on a run. "Wait," cried the rooster. "Why do you run? The dogs are friends of yours now!"

"Yes," answered the fox. "But they might not have heard the news. Besides, I have a very important errand that I had almost forgotten about." The rooster smiled as he buried his head in his feathers and went to sleep, for he had succeeded in outwitting a very crafty enemy.

Moral: The trickster is easily tricked.

The Wolf and the Shepherd

A wolf had been prowling around a flock of sheep for a long time, and the shepherd watched very anxiously to prevent him from carrying off a lamb. But the wolf did not try to do any harm. Instead, he seemed to be helping the shepherd take care of the sheep. At last, the shepherd got so used to seeing the wolf around that he forgot how wicked he could be. One day he even went so far as to leave his flock in the wolf's care while he went on an errand. But when he came back and saw how many of the flock had been killed and carried off, he knew how foolish to trust a wolf.

Moral: Once a wolf, always a wolf.

The Lion and the Mouse

A lion lay asleep in the forest, his great head resting on his paws. A timid little mouse came upon him unexpectedly, and in her fright and haste to get away, she ran across the lion's nose. Roused from his nap, the lion laid his huge paw angrily on the tiny creature to kill her. "Spare me!" begged the poor mouse. "Please let me go and someday I will surely repay you." The lion was much amused to think that a mouse could ever help him. But he was generous and let the mouse go. Some days later, while stalking his prey in the forest, the lion was caught in the coils of a hunter's net. Unable to free himself, he filled the forest with his angry roaring. The mouse knew the voice and quickly found the lion struggling in the net. Running to one of the great ropes that bound him, she gnawed it until it parted, and soon the lion was free. "You laughed when I said I would repay you," said the mouse. "Now you see that even a mouse can help a lion."

Moral: A kindness is never wasted.

The Dogs and the Fox

Some dogs found the skin of a lion and furiously began to tear it with their teeth. A fox chanced to see them and laughed scornfully. "If that lion had been alive," he said, "it would have been a very different story. He would have made you feel how much sharper his claws are than your teeth."

Moral: It is easy but contemptible to kick a man that is down.

The Sick Stag

A stag had fallen sick. He had just enough strength to gather some food and find a quiet clearing in the woods, where he lay down to wait until his strength should return. The animals heard about the stag's illness and came to ask after his health. Of course, they were all hungry, and helped themselves freely to the stag's food; and as you would expect, the stag soon starved to death.

Moral: Goodwill is worth nothing unless it is accompanied by good acts.

The Eagle and the Fox

An eagle and a fox formed an intimate friendship and decided to live near each other. The eagle built her nest in the branches of a tall tree, while the fox crept into the underwood and there produced her young. Not long after they had agreed upon this plan, the eagle, being in want of provision for her young ones, swooped down while the fox was out, seized upon one of the little cubs, and feasted herself and her brood. The fox discovered on her return what had happened but was less grieved for the death of her young than for her inability to avenge them. A just retribution, however, quickly fell upon the eagle. While hovering near an altar on which some villagers were sacrificing a goat, she seized a piece of the meat and carried it, along with a burning cinder, to her nest. A strong breeze soon fanned the spark into a flame and the eaglets, as yet unfledged and helpless, were roasted in their nest and dropped down dead at the bottom of the tree. There, in the sight of the eagle, the fox gobbled them up.

Moral: Hunger can turn friends into enemies.

The Laborer and the Nightingale

A laborer lay listening to a nightingale's song throughout the summer night. So pleased was he with it that the next night he set a trap for it and captured it. "Now that I have caught you," he cried, "you shall always sing to me."

"We nightingales never sing in a cage," said the bird.

"Then I'll eat you," said the laborer. "I have always heard it said that nightingale on toast is a dainty morsel."

"No, kill me not," said the nightingale, "but let be me free, and I'll tell you three things worth far more than my poor body."

The laborer let him loose, and the nightingale flew up to a branch of a tree and said, "Never believe a captive's promise; that's one thing. Then again, keep what you have. And the third piece of advice is this: Sorrow not over what is lost forever." Then the songbird flew away.

Moral: People should never trust a promise made under pressure.

Part III

Using Nontraditional Formats

"Show me that you've read it."

Low on drudgery but high on thought, the following five techniques offer students a variety of ways to share their mental process while reading, writing, thinking, and speaking.

These strategies appeal not only to reading and language arts teachers who might feel ready for some variety, but they're also the perfect choice for teachers of other disciplines who would rather not ask their students to write essays on a regular basis. And unlike ineffective methods (such as the infamous reading guides), these don't lend themselves to copied answers, plagiarized from the internet.

Once students have learned how to do these five strategies, it's easy to give them a choice. And students do their best work when they get to make choices—as do teachers.

Strategy 1 (QA12345) produces a dialogue for proofreading aloud.

Strategy 2 (Cubing Infoshots) generates and synthesizes information using relationships from the SAT analogies.

Strategy 3 (Ba-da-bings) creates a verbal visual of a moment.

Strategy 4 (Three-Things Response) creates a comforting self-generated worksheet of no-fail thinking.

Strategy 5 (One-Liners) produces a cartoon with five thoughts.

Five Handy Ways to Respond to Reading

QA12345 Dialogue

| Q | A | How do you know? | What does that mean? | How else do you know? | What does that mean? | So your answer is? |

Cubing Infoshots

| Define it | Describe it | What is it used for? | What is it similar to? | What can it cause? | What it will transform into |

Ba-da-bings

| What you were doing | What you saw | What you knew then |

Three-Things Response

| Three things I noticed | Three things I wonder | Significant vocabulary | Best line, illustrated |

One-Liners

| Text | (Paraphrase) | Subtext | Truism | Dramatic analysis |

USING THESE STRATEGIES IN THE CONTENT AREAS

Imagine questions in any content area, such as the social studies question, "Explain one significant result of the presidential election of 1828." See the five different ways to show that you understand (below):

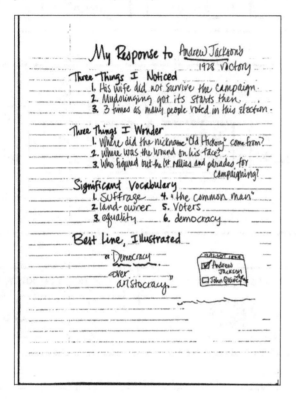

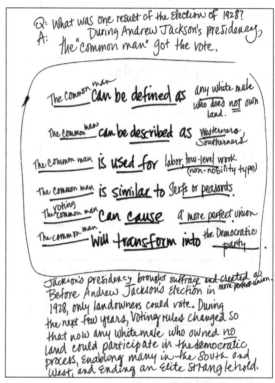

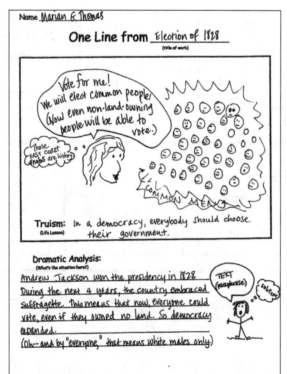

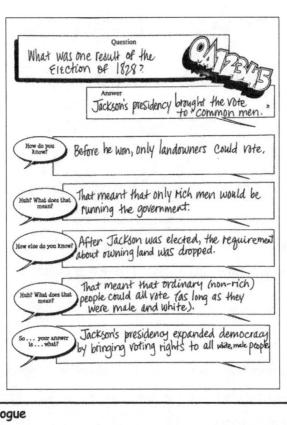

QA12345 Dialogue

| Q | A | How do you know? | Huh? What does that mean? | How else do you know? | Huh? What does that mean? | So ... your answer is ...? |

Ba-da-bings

| What your feet were doing | What you saw | What you knew then |

Cubing Infoshots

| Define it | Describe it | What is it used for? | What is it similar to? | What it can cause? | What it will transform into |

Three Things Response

| Three things I noticed | Three things I wonder | Significant vocabulary | Best line, illustrated |

One-Liners

| Text | (Paraphrase) | Subtext | Truism | Dramatic analysis |

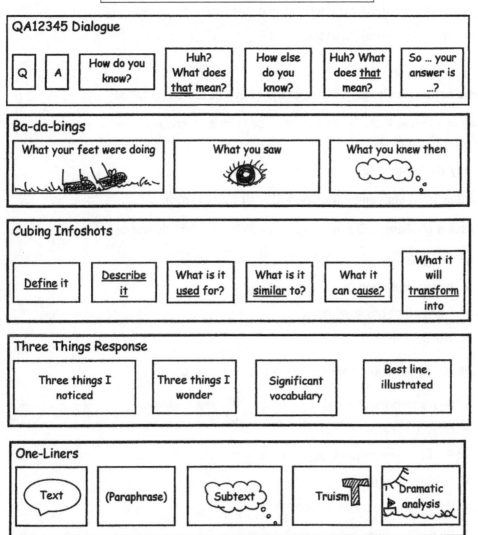

If students use these, it becomes effortless to give them choices.

SHOW ME YOU DID YOUR READING

Show That You Read Your Assignment

Required

Choose one:

- Pick any structure and write a quick kernel essay.
- Write a thank-you letter from one character to another.
- Pick any other message structure and have one character write to another.
- Write a ba-da-bing sentence as a character.
- Do a one-liner.
- Write a three-things response.
- Draw a scene from the story and write a truism as a caption.
- Write and answer a short-answer question.
- Write an 11-minute essay.

Optional

Combination challenge: Do two of the above at the same time.

Craft challenge: Include (and color-code with a legend) any two choices of craft from our writer's toolbox.

Brevity challenge: Use no more than 35 words.

Random word challenge: Include today's random word: _____.

Omission challenge: Choose one of the following and do *not* use it in your writing:

- Plural words
- Words ending in *y*
- Words that begin with *t*
- Words with three syllables

Unmitigated Scholar Challenge: Sprinkle in any of these:

- SAT vocabulary words
- Obscure rhetorical devices
- Shakespearean phrases
- Subordinate clauses
- References to physics theories
- Beyoncé lyrics

LESSON 6. THE QA12345 DIALOGUE

6

"Explain your answer fully."

Sometimes students earn low grades on short-answer questions (also called **text-based questions** or **constructed-response questions**) on tests because they didn't answer the question fully. Maybe they read the selection and understood it well but as they wrote their response, their words drifted away from answering the question. Or maybe they answered the question but didn't show the evidence that helped them form the answer.

This exercise turns the question–answer process into a dialogue, a real dialogue between two humans. When students hear one person asking, "What time is it?" and another human answering, "We always eat early," their ears know that the answer didn't match the question at all. When it comes to content, ears proofread best.

Step 1. Teach them the dialogue.

1. Write the QA12345 script on the screen or board so that everyone can see it.

2. Get a volunteer to stand beside you.

3. Tell that volunteer that you're going to ask questions; they should answer each question you ask using a truthful, complete sentence.

4. Tell the volunteer that everyone in the room is a lifeline and will help if they need it.

5. Ask the volunteer a question from the practice questions below.

6. Continue with the script to the end.

7. Get a different volunteer and a different question and repeat the same script.

8. Ask students to copy the QA12345 script into their journals.

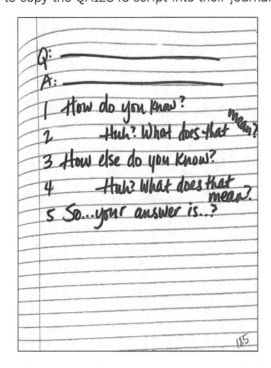

Step 2. Use the dialogue to answer any open-ended question about a text.

Students do the following:

1. Read any text.

2. Use the question stems from Lessons 4 or 5 to create a question.

3. Use QA12345 to write answers.

4. Pick a partner to be the questioner and perform the dialogue.

QA12345 SCRIPT

Question: _____

Answer: _____

1. How do you know?
2. What does that mean?
3. How else do you know?
4. What does that mean?
5. So, your answer is . . . what?

PRACTICE QUESTIONS

What is your name?

What color are your eyes?

Is it hot outside?

How did you get here today?

Is it raining right now?

What is your mom's name?

Which state do you live in?

Where were you born?

What shoes are you wearing?

What color is your hair?

What color is the sky?

What is your favorite color?

When is your birthday?

How many stars are on the United States flag?

What is your favorite dessert?

How many fingers are on your left hand?

What's one thing you can buy at McDonalds?

What color are your fingernails?

STUDENT SAMPLES

QA12345: "The Fox and the Leopard"
Tatum George, Grade 11

Q: *Why did the fox say the leopard had an unattractive mind?*

A: The fox believes that relying on your looks does not prove you are better than others.

1. *How do you know?*

   The fox told the leopard that a fine mind is better than a fine coat.

2. *What does that mean?*

   It means the fox values smarts over beauty.

3. *How else do you know?*

   The leopard called the fox ordinary looking.

4. *What does that mean?*

   It means the leopard only cares about his looks and uses them to make people feel less than him.

5. *So, your answer is . . . what?*

   The fox used his wit to prove to the leopard that looks mean nothing without smarts.

QA12345: *Sky-High Dreams*
Madeleine Kristof, Grade 2

Q. *What was this book mostly about?*

A. It was mostly about a boy named Hank and the Great Depression.

1. *How do you know?*

   Hank was sad because he had to move in with his cousins when his dad lost his job and couldn't pay the rent.

2. *What does that mean?*

   It said it was 1930 and I read in two other books that people were losing their jobs because of a drought in the Great Depression.

3. *How else do you know?*

   I know Hank didn't smile and even the illustrations had sad dull colors like black, gray, and some yellow.

4. *What does that mean?*

   The Great Depression was a hard time but some happy times because Hank got cheered up watching them construct the Empire State Building.

5. *So, your answer is . . . what?*

   This book must be historical fiction because the Empire State Building is still standing!

QA12345: *The Call of the Wild*
Adriana Trujillo, Grade 6

Q: *How does Buck change in* The Call of the Wild?

A. He goes from a spoiled house dog to the leader of a wolf pack.

1. *How do you know?*

   In the beginning of the book, he was always taken care of.

2. *What does that mean?*

   Judge Miller fed him, and on colder nights, he slept with the judge in his bed.

3. *How else do you know?*

   At the end, he lived with a wolf pack and he got respect from the other wolves.

4. *What does that mean?*

   They took his barked orders and were always under his command.

5. *So, how does Buck change?*

   He goes from a strong tame dog to a mighty wild wolf.

QA12345: "She Inherits His Steady Hand"
Michelle A. Douglas, adult

Michelle

Q What can the reader conclude from the action in lines 4-6?

Question	Answer	How do you know?	What does that mean?	How else do you know?	What does that mean?	So, your answer o.3

A In lines 4-6, the reader can conclude that the five-year-old granddaughter is taking care of her grandfather.

1 I know this because the young girl is feeding him with a spoon.

Evidence in #1 & #3

2 This means he has lost his ability to feed himself and now depends on another person's assistance to be able to eat.

3 I also know that he is "opening his mouth to be fed like a bird" which reveals his loss of independence.

4 This means his granddaughter is taking on the mother role as she feeds him like a baby bird.

5 The action of feeding her grandfather conveys the diminishing Nana's loss of independence.

QA12345: Paul Erickson's comic book page
Claudia Wilson, adult

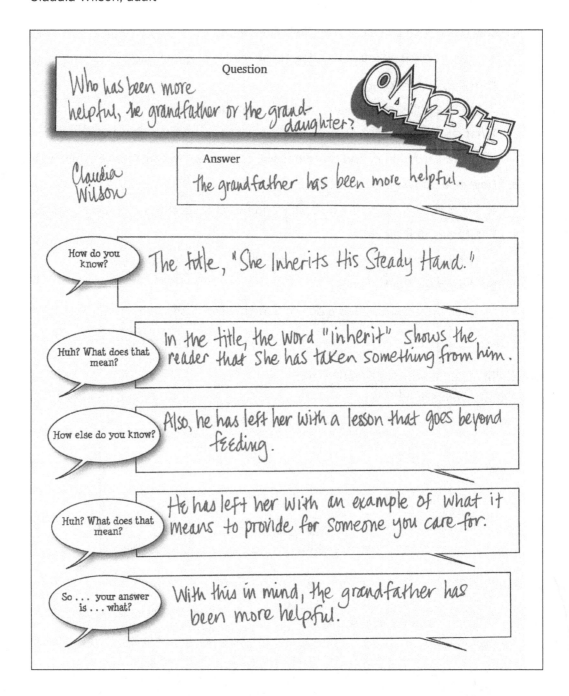

Variation: Delete the question and now you have a handy structure for argument.

Extension: To strengthen the answers, delete repetitions and combine sentences.

7

LESSON 7. INFOSHOT (CUBING): SHOW WHAT YOU KNOW

When asked to show what they know about something, students don't often know how to frame an answer.

"What do you know about paramecium?"

"They're little."

"Can you tell more about paramecium?"

"They're really, really little."

Wouldn't it be nice if they answered, "A paramecium is a single-celled organism shaped like a slipper. Its body is covered in cilia, which it uses to propel itself in water. Scientists consider it like a 'white rat' because studying it helps them understand biological processes."

This is an example of a six-in-one infoshot, but students can make shorter ones such as a three-in-one infoshot. It's teachable.

Adapted from Elizabeth Cowan's (1980) cubing strategy in her book *Writing*, this technique gives students a concrete method for generating a lot of material about a word or concept. Then they combine it all and pare it down to a synthesized explanation.

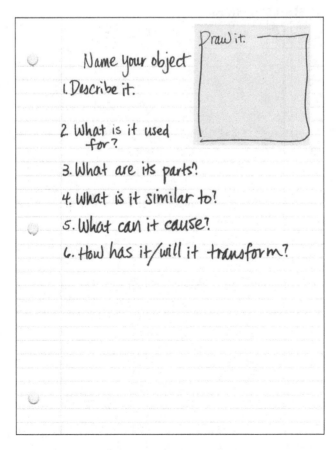

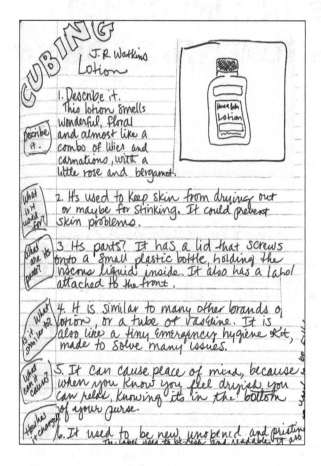

Practice infoshots with concrete life objects first.

You can either have students free write for all six parts or write simple sentence infoshots, using the stem sentences.

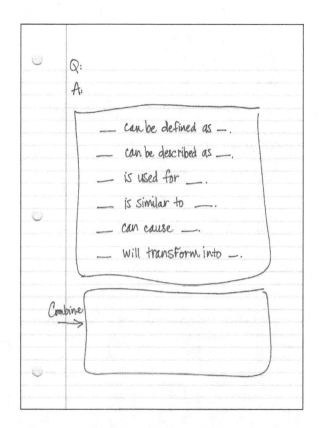

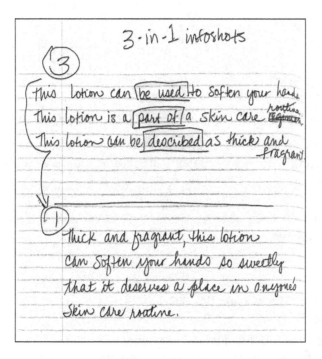

After exploring this process, try it with terms or words from the students' learning. It works great with abstract concepts from a text.

Step 1. Read or listen to a fable.

Step 2. Pick a key word from the text. Choose a word you like; nouns work best.

Step 3. Use the template below to write infoshot sentences. Use it to fill in the first blank in each sentence. Fill in the last blank in each sentence with whatever makes sense to you.

Step 4. Combine the infoshot sentences to make a paragraph that you like. You may change, omit, add, or rearrange the words.

Step 5. Share.

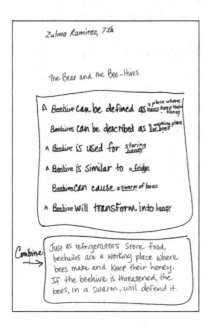

STUDENT SAMPLES

Three-in-One Infoshot: "The Lion and the Three Bulls"
Katelyn Blackwell, Grade 7

1. A quarrel can be defined as a disagreement where people often get very angry.
2. A quarrel is similar to an argument.
3. Quarrels can cause people to get distracted by their own problems and ignore danger.

Combined:
When people quarrel or have disagreements, their anger distracts them so much that they might ignore danger.

Six-in-One Infoshot: "The Kid and the Wolf"
Murad Haji, Grade 7

1. Friskiness can be defined as full of energy.
2. Frisky can be described as playful or energetic.
3. Friskiness is used to describe puppies that still want to play.
4. Frisky is similar to jumpy.
5. Friskiness can cause trouble.
6. Friskiness will transform into mischief.

Combined:
As long as someone feels frisky, jumpy, or energetic, they will probably still want to play, which can turn into mischief and cause trouble.

Student Samples From Other Subjects

Six-in-One Infoshot: Eggshells
Alex Espinosa, Grade 4

1. Eggshells can be defined as hard waste.
2. Eggshells can be described as easily broken.
3. Eggshells can be used as food for other organisms.
4. Eggshells are similar to other food waste.
5. Eggshells can cause plants to grow.
6. Eggshells will transform into pure energy.

Combined:
Are your plants not growing well? Eggshells can cause plants to grow better. When composted, eggshells will convert into energy and are similar to other food waste. They can become food for other organisms. They can also be defined as easily broken solid waste.

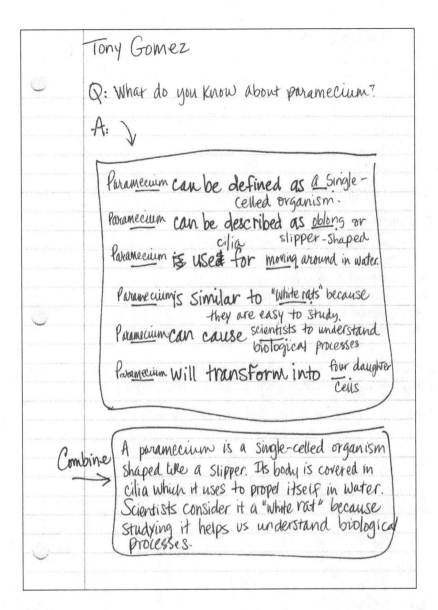

Tony Gomez

Q: What do you know about paramecium?

A: ↓

Paramecium can be defined as a single-celled organism.
Paramecium can be described as oblong or slipper-shaped
Paramecium is used for moving around in water.
                    cilia

Paramecium is similar to "white rats" because they are easy to study.
Paramecium can cause scientists to understand biological processes
Paramecium will transform into four daughter cells

Combine → A paramecium is a single-celled organism shaped like a slipper. Its body is covered in cilia which it uses to propel itself in water. Scientists consider it a "white rat" because studying it helps us understand biological processes.

Tips: In order to narrow down a topic, you can also begin with a quick list, as our friend Don did here:

Quick list:
Books that have changed you:

1. *Moby Dick*
2. *Dr. Zhivago*
3. *The Covenant*

Tangible things important in your life:

4. my grandson
5. my daughters
6. nature

Qualities important in a friend:

7. honesty
8. empathy
9. directness

Mysteries of the world (things that perplex you):

10. the tides
11. the Mariana Trench
12. the northern lights

Next, choose one thing from the list to use for a six-in-one infoshot.

Six-in-One Infoshot:

1. My grandson can be defined as curious.
2. My grandson can be described as high-energy.
3. My grandson is used for love.
4. My grandson is similar to me.
5. My grandson can cause chaos
6. My grandson will transform into a gentleman.

Combined:

My grandson is curious, high-energy, and, like me, causes chaos wherever he goes. Despite this, the love he receives will transform him into a gentleman.

Extensions: You can use or create graphics like these to help.

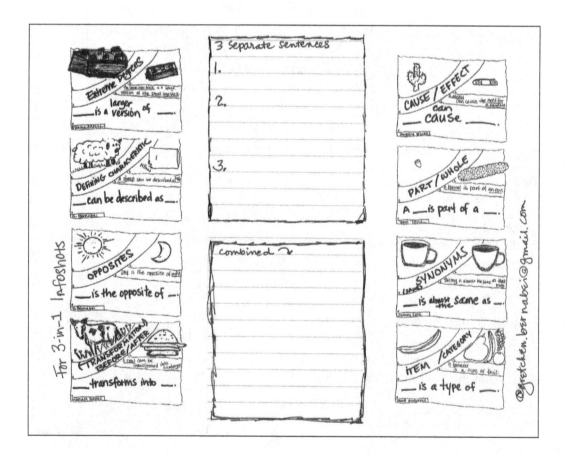

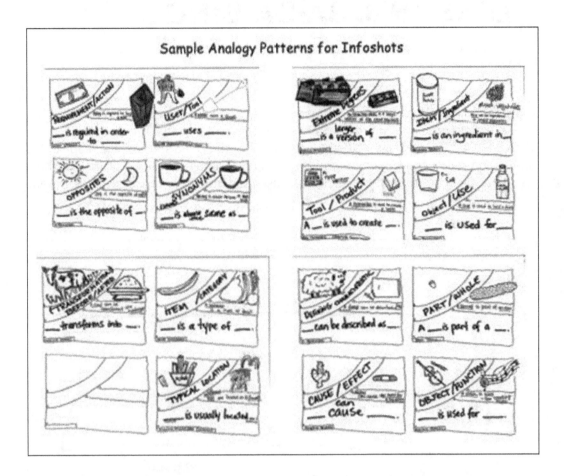

Sample Analogy Patterns for Infoshots

Tips: This exercise is right at home in a journal or it makes a great exit slip. It's a perfect way for students to gain and show understanding of new vocabulary or concepts from any content area.

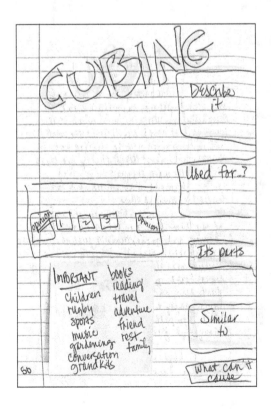

CUBING

Describe it

Used for...?

Opinion [1] [2] [3] Opinion

Its parts

Similar to

What can't cause

IMPORTANT books
Children reading
rugby travel
sports adventure
music friend
gardening rest
conversation family
grandkids

50

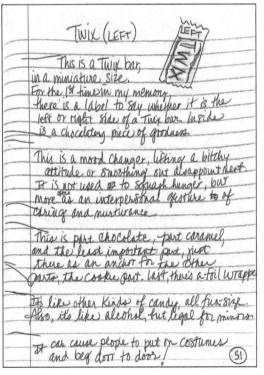

TWIX (LEFT)

This is a Twix bar, in a miniature size. For the 1st time in my memory, there is a label to say whether it is the left or right side of a Twix bar. Inside is a chocolatey piece of goodness

This is a mood changer, lifting a bitchy attitude or smoothing out disappointment. It is not used to squash hunger, but more as an interpersonal gesture of caring and nurturance.

This is part chocolate, part caramel, and the least important part, just there as an anchor for the other parts, the cookie part. Last, there's a foil wrapper

Its like other kinds of candy, all fun-size. Also, it's like alcohol, but legal for minors

It can cause people to put on costumes and beg door to door!

51

8

LESSON 8. BA-DA-BING

A writer can clearly see what's in their mind's eye; a reader cannot. As writers, we have difficulty remembering this, a condition Steven Pinker (2014) calls "the curse of knowledge." Ba-da-bings help students write for the mind's eye of the reader. This simple and quick one-sentence strategy produces wonderful (and original!) writing. It's useful for practical exit slips. You can ask students to write ba-da-bings for any content area.

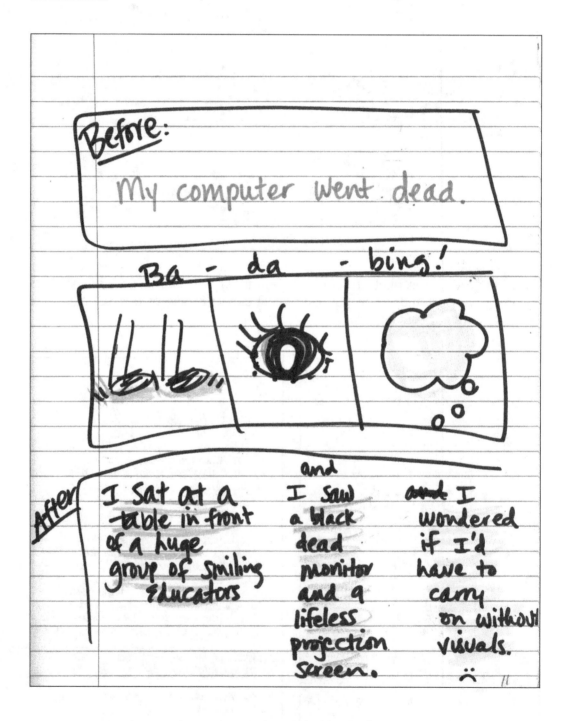

When writing about themselves:

1. Ask students to write a sentence about one moment when something happened to them.

2. Show them the ba-da-bing icons and explain the three parts of the sentence—what I did, what I saw, and what I thought—all at the same moment.

3. Write a ba-da-bing version of the sentence they wrote.

4. Share and compare.

When writing in response to text:

1. Read or listen to a fable.

2. Pick a moment in the story.

3. Write a ba-da-bing sentence for that moment by telling these three things: what I did, what I saw, and what I thought.

Ba-da-bing: 1st Person (as me or as a character)		
What I did	What I saw	What I thought

4. Listen to each other's ba-da-bings.

STUDENT SAMPLES

Ba-da-bing: "The Lion and the Three Bulls"

I was one of the bulls. I was in a separate corner. I heard whining coming from the other corners. I turned and saw the other bulls getting slaughtered. I regretted parting ways with the other bulls.

—Aiden Fogle, Grade 7

The lion's toes brushed the sandy ground with anticipation as his eyes wavered on the many bulls feasting. His body tickled, the need for food beginning to devour him. This wasn't his fault; it was his nature.

—Regan Jackson, Grade 7

My paws slowly and surely stepped on the grass, a quiet crunch with each movement. My eyes locked on the bulls. But there was something different, usually tight together as one, they were far apart. I thought to myself, now is my chance.

—Ainsley Mattson, Grade 7

I was lying in my corner eating my hay when I saw a lion watching me. I knew that it was my last meal. Watching my family getting guzzled and gulped, I hurried for the river but was too late. I found myself in the river of the lion's stomach.

—Mallory Smith, Grade 7

I was down low in the grass when I saw that the tasty bulls were not together. Then I thought, "Pounce!"

—Isaac Gelfond, Grade 7

Ba-da-bing: "The Fox and the Pheasants"

The last thing my foot did was shiver on the branch. The last thing I thought was, "Dearest me! What is that fox doing?" My final sight was the fox's mouth wide open.
—Zachary Ballard, Grade 7

One day I was sitting on a branch minding my own business when I saw a fox start to dance on his hind legs. He was dancing wildly, and I didn't know why I couldn't look away, and then in a matter of seconds, I saw myself falling in the fox's mouth.
—Madilyn Ricker, Grade 7

Ba-da-bing: "The Bear and the Beehives"

Nosing around the foreboding woods, I smelled the sweet aroma of honey. Hmmm, I thought, bees!

—Anna Kate Roberts, Grade 7

I was walking cautiously around the trees, looking for the juicy berries. And that's when I found the nest of the swarm of bees on a fallen tree! A smile began to form on my face, thinking about eating that delicious, sweet honey.

—Sophia Lee, Grade 7

One day I was flying to my hive from the clover fields when I saw a bear snooping around my hive, so I stung him. Then suddenly he grew angry and tried to destroy my hive. I felt invigorated and thought to myself, no one will ever defeat me.

—Tinsley Kure, Grade 7

Here is an example from a fairy tale:

Ba-da-bing: "The Frog Prince"

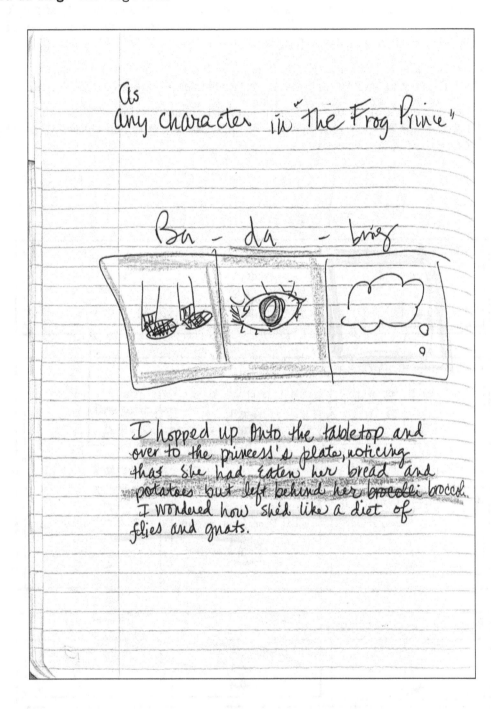

Tips:

As our friend Harry Noden (2011) says, "When we're giving students directions for something complex, we have to oversimplify it at first." Whenever a student asks, "Would it be all right if I wrote this as more than one sentence?" you say, "Hmm. Try it and let's see how that works!" And of course, it will be fine.

At first, students may adhere to the verbs *walked*, *saw*, and *thought*. As soon as you show delight in their variations, they will become more relaxed and have more fun choosing their words.

Extensions:

- If you collect first person ba-da-bing sentences as exit strips, you could choose several to show the next day as warm-ups. You read the sentence aloud and follow it with "Who am I?" It's fun and it teaches students to plant context clues as they direct the mind's eye of the reader.

- Once students become adept at writing ba-da-bings, play with any of the variations below to teach dramatic irony, character change, theme—the works.

- Celebrate (with praise, extra credit, confetti, whatever works) when you notice ba-da-bings in their reading. See the first sentence in *The Outsiders* or *The Glass Castle*, for example.

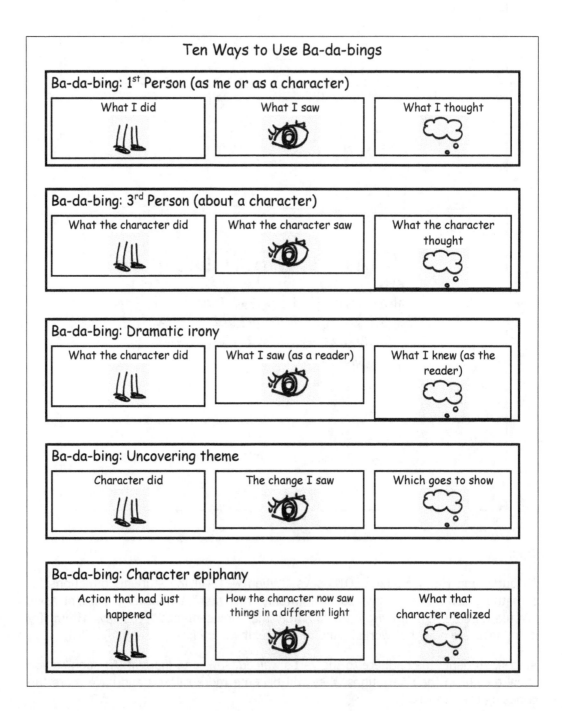

Ten Ways to Use Ba-da-bings

Ba-da-bing: 1ˢᵗ Person (as me or as a character)

| What I did | What I saw | What I thought |

Ba-da-bing: 3ʳᵈ Person (about a character)

| What the character did | What the character saw | What the character thought |

Ba-da-bing: Dramatic irony

| What the character did | What I saw (as a reader) | What I knew (as the reader) |

Ba-da-bing: Uncovering theme

| Character did | The change I saw | Which goes to show |

Ba-da-bing: Character epiphany

| Action that had just happened | How the character now saw things in a different light | What that character realized |

Ba-da-bing: Reader as paparazzi watching for a conflict

One character did this	A different character saw this	And the reader knew this

Ba-da-bing: A moment of regret

At an important moment, what the character did **not** do	What the character saw	What the reader suspected

Ba-da-bing: Character blind spot

The character did this	The character saw this	What the character did not know

Ba-da-bing: Tough decision

The character thought	This made the character do this	The reader noticed	Which told me this

Ba-da-bing: Spin (or one way to see an issue)

What happened	What the author let you see/present to you	What that leads you to think

Ba-da-bing Blanks

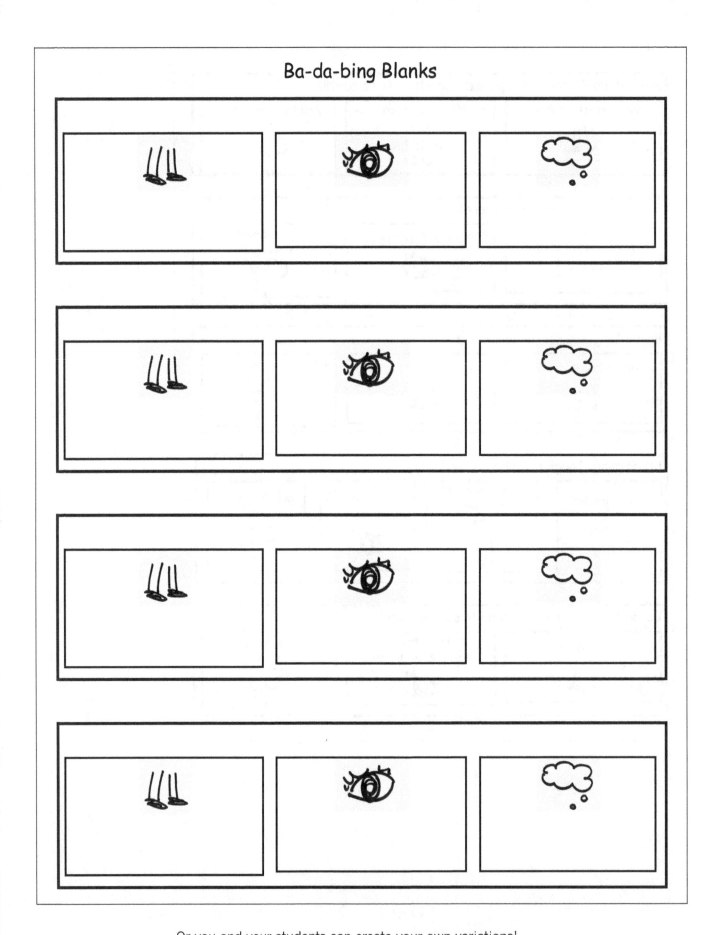

Or you and your students can create your own variations!

LESSON 9. THREE-THINGS RESPONSE

9

This practice helps to curb the "just tell me what to write to make an A" tendency that plagues some students by asking them instead to draw from their own thoughts in a very concrete format. We can tell them curiosity is valuable, but if we don't back that up in the form of payment (which, at school, is grades), then it's not true in our classrooms.

Students can use this form to write a response to anything: a story, a conversation, lunch, the counselor's visit—anything. It's a great prelude to a discussion ("Let's hear one thing you noticed") where even the shy students can participate. It also comes in handy when there's a substitute or when a student needs to earn credit for some makeup work or to bring up a grade.

Step 1. Copy the template.

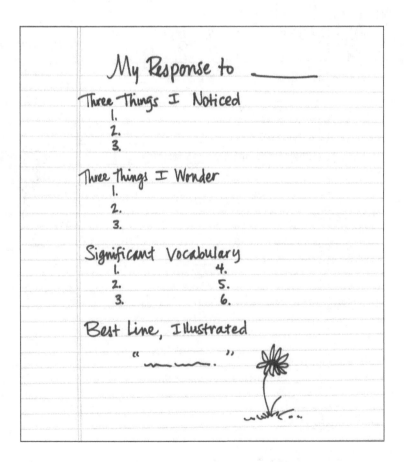

Step 2. Read the following example aloud with students.

Notice that

- the first two sections are complete sentences.
- the third section lists words that you thought were important for any reason (even if you just liked those words).
- the fourth section could be any phrase or sentence with some kind of illustration.

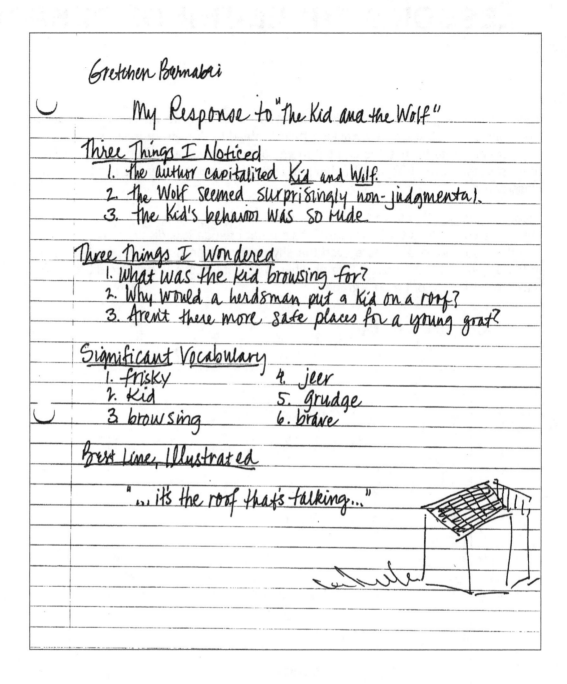

Gretchen Bernabei

My Response to "The Kid and the Wolf"

Three Things I Noticed
1. The author capitalized Kid and Wolf.
2. The Wolf seemed surprisingly non-judgmental.
3. The Kid's behavior was so rude.

Three Things I Wondered
1. What was the Kid browsing for?
2. Why would a herdsman put a Kid on a roof?
3. Aren't there more safe places for a young goat?

Significant Vocabulary
1. frisky   4. jeer
2. Kid   5. grudge
3. browsing   6. brave

Best Line, Illustrated

"... it's the roof that's talking..."

Step 3. Read a fable.

Step 4. Fill in the template with your thoughts.

Step 5. Share your work with a partner or group.

Tip: Ask students to copy the template into their writer's notebooks or journals and keep a copy posted in your room. Then students can generate a three-things response to anything they read, do, learn, or experience.

STUDENT SAMPLES

Three-Things Response: "The Ant and the Grasshopper"

My Response to: The Ants and the Grasshopper

Three things I noticed

1. The grasshopper seemed lazy.
2. The ants were hard workers.
3. The ants were suprised that the grasshopper didn't get food for the winter.

Three Things I wondered

1. Why didn't the grasshopper get food for the winter when it was time?
2. Why didn't the ants just give him some food?
3. What will happen to the grasshopper later?

Significant Vocabulary

1. Humbly
2. Idleness
3. Disgust
4. Fiddle
5. Begged
6. Stored

Best Line, Illustrated

"I was so busy making music that before I knew it the summer was gone."

—Zinnia Briseño, Grade 3

Berlyn E. Cash

My Response to The donkey and the lap dog.

Three things I noticed

1. The donkey was feeling a lot of envy towards the dog.
2. The donkey had a lot of confidence that his plan would work.
3. When the donkey was sad it was understandable.

Three things I wonder

1. I wonder if the master really did appreciate the donkey.
2. I wonder if the dog knew of the donkey's sadness.
3. I wonder if the master loved the donkey.

Significant Vocabulary

1. imitate   3. Movin   5 danger
2. discontent   4. giddily   6. attention

Best line Illustrated

"All he had to do... was act like dog."

—Berlyn Cash, Grade 3

Three-Things Response: Hamlet's speech to the actors in *Hamlet*

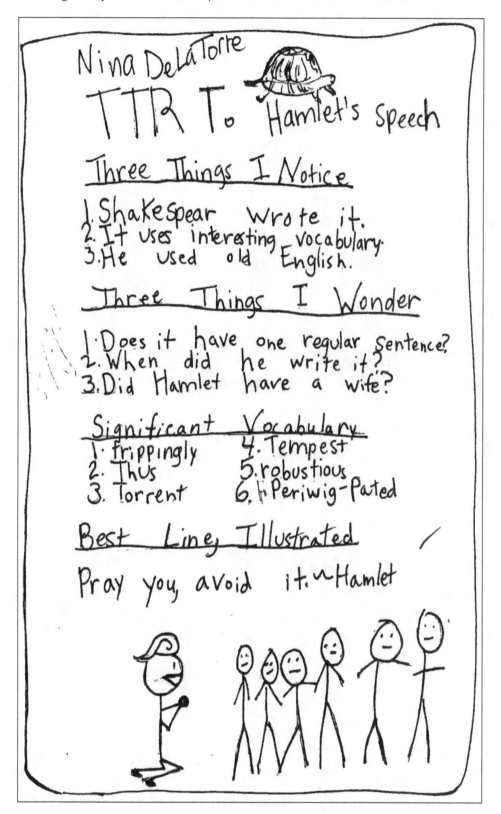

Nina DeLaTorre

TTRT. Hamlet's Speech

Three Things I Notice

1. Shakespear wrote it.
2. It uses interesting vocabulary.
3. He used old English.

Three Things I Wonder

1. Does it have one regular sentence?
2. When did he write it?
3. Did Hamlet have a wife?

Significant Vocabulary
1. trippingly   4. Tempest
2. Thus   5. robustious
3. Torrent   6. Periwig-Pated

Best Line, Illustrated

Pray you, avoid it. ~Hamlet

—Nina De La Torre, Grade 7

Atticus
H. Stephen

Three things Response:
(The Porcupine and the Snakes)

Three things I noticed:
1) The porcupine did not have ill intentions
   when looking for a home.
2) The Snakes were very Kind and considerate.
3) The Porcupine seemed oblivious more than
   he seemed mean.

Three things I wonder:
1) If there was a bigger home for the porcupine
   nearby
2) If a solution could be made between
   the porcupine and snakes
3) Where the snakes went after they left

Significant Vocab:
- Used sophisticated language like "Kindly
  Consented", "well satisfied", and "politely
  escorted".

Best Line Illustrated:
- "To save their skins, the Snakes had to look
  for another home."

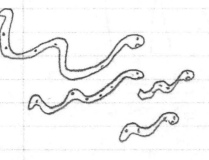
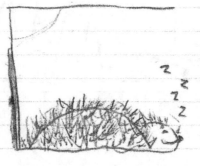

—Atticus Stephen Grade 11

Too often, students don't see a connection between text and people. They don't imagine that *text* is words uttered by a human person, sometimes in writing and sometimes out loud. This activity converts text to speech, where students literally draw the context, imagine the unspoken thoughts of the speaker, and write a life lesson for that moment. We call these *one-liners*. They not only make a beautiful display on a wall but they also show complex cognitive understanding of a text.

- **Step 1.** Read or listen to a fable.

- **Step 2**. Choose one thing someone said in the story.

- **Step 3.** Use the one-liner template to draw and write the following:
  - Draw the character and their surroundings.
  - Text: Draw a word bubble and write their words in it.
  - Paraphrase: Inside the word bubble, put the text into simple words. Use parentheses around your paraphrase.
  - Subtext: Inside a thought bubble, write what that character is thinking.
  - Truism: Write a life lesson for this moment.
  - Dramatic analysis: What's the situation at this moment? Where is it happening? Who are the characters? What's the problem?

Tip: Only one character will have word bubbles or thought bubbles. A one-liner means it's just one line—one utterance from one character—not a dialogue. It freezes the action.

One-Liner: "The Bear and the Beehives"

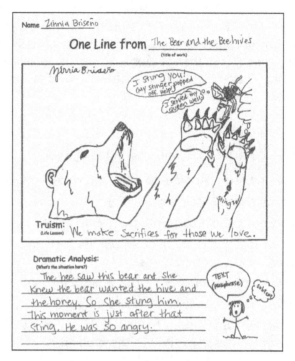

—Zinnia Briseño, Grade 3

One-Liner: *The Crucible*

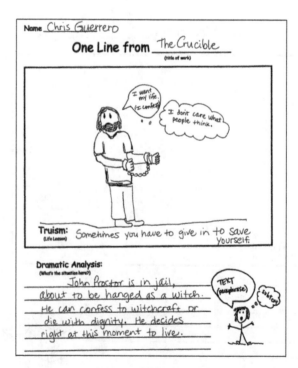

—Chris Guerrero, Grade 10

The Milkmaid and Her Pot of Milk

A milkmaid had been out to milk the cows and was returning from the field with the shining milk pail balanced nicely on her head. As she walked along, her pretty head was busy with plans for the days to come. "This good, rich milk," she mused, "will give me plenty of cream to churn. The butter I make I will take to market, and with the money I get for it, I will buy a lot of eggs for hatching. How nice it will be when they are all hatched and the yard is full of fine young chicks. Then when May Day comes, I will sell them, and with the money, I'll buy a lovely new dress to wear to the fair. All the young men will look at me. They will come and try to propose to me—but I shall very quickly send them about their business!" As she thought of how she would settle that matter, she tossed her head scornfully and down fell the pail of milk to the ground. All the milk flowed out, and with it vanished butter and eggs and chicks and a new dress and all the milkmaid's pride.

Moral: It's unwise to count your chickens before they are hatched.

The Donkey and the Lapdog

There was once a donkey whose master also owned a lapdog. This dog was a favorite and received many a pat and kind word from his master as well as choice bits from his plate. Every day, the dog would run to meet the master, frisking playfully about and leaping up to lick his hands and face. All this the donkey saw with much discontent. Though he was well fed, he had much work to do; besides, the master hardly ever took any notice of him. Now the jealous donkey got it into his silly head that all he had to do to win his master's favor was to act like the dog. So one day, he left his stable and clattered eagerly into the house. Finding his master seated at the dinner table, he kicked up his heels and, with a loud bray, pranced giddily around the table, upsetting it as he did so. Then he planted his forefeet on his master's knees and rolled out his tongue to lick the master's face, as he had seen the dog do. But his weight upset the chair, and donkey and man rolled over together in the pile of broken dishes from the table. The master was much alarmed at the strange behavior of the donkey and, calling for help, soon attracted the attention of the servants. When they saw the danger the master was in from the clumsy beast, they set upon the donkey and drove him back to the stable with kicks and blows. There they left him to mourn the foolishness that had brought him nothing but a sound beating.

Moral: It is better to be true to your own character and nature than to imitate others.

The Stag and His Reflection

A stag, drinking from a crystal spring, saw himself mirrored in the clear water. He greatly admired the graceful arch of his antlers, but he was very much ashamed of his spindling legs. "How can it be," he sighed, "that I should be cursed with such legs when I have so magnificent a crown?" At that moment, he scented a panther and in an instant was bounding away through the forest. But as he ran, his wide-spreading antlers caught in the branches of the trees, and soon the panther overtook him. Then the stag perceived that the legs of which he was so ashamed would have saved him had it not been for the useless ornaments on his head.

Moral: What is most truly valuable is often despised.

The Owl and the Grasshopper

An owl who was sitting in a hollow tree, dozing away a summer's afternoon, was very much disturbed by a rogue of a grasshopper singing in the grass beneath. So far from keeping quiet or moving away at the request of the owl, the grasshopper sang all the more and called her an old blinker who only came out at night when all honest people had gone to bed. The owl waited in silence for a time and then artfully addressed the grasshopper as follows: "Well, my dear, if one cannot be allowed to sleep, it is something to be kept awake by such a pleasant voice. And now that I think of it, I have a bottle of delicious nectar. If you will come up, you shall have a drop." The silly grasshopper came hopping up to the owl, who at once caught and killed him and finished her nap in comfort.

Moral: Flattery is not proof of admiration.

The Donkey and His Masters

A certain donkey that belonged to a gardener was weary of carrying heavy burdens and prayed to Jupiter to give him a new master. Jupiter granted his prayer and gave him for a master a tilemaker, who made him carry heavier burdens than before. Again he came to Jupiter and besought him to grant him a milder master or, at any rate, a different one. The god, laughing at his folly, thereupon gave him over to a tanner. The donkey was worked harder than ever and soon upbraided himself for his stupidity. "Now," he said, "I have a master who not only beats me while I live but who will not spare my hide even when I am dead."

Moral: It's better to be content with what you have.

The Ants and the Grasshopper

One bright day in late autumn, a family of ants were bustling about in the warm sunshine, drying out the grain they had stored up during the summer, when a starving grasshopper, his fiddle under his arm, came up and humbly begged for a bite to eat. "What?" cried the ants in surprise. "Haven't you stored anything away for the winter? What in the world were you doing all summer?"

"I didn't have time to store up any food," whined the grasshopper. "I was so busy making music that before I knew it, the summer was gone."

The ants shrugged their shoulders in disgust. "Making music, were you?" they cried. "Very well; now dance!" And they turned their backs on the grasshopper and went on with their work.

Moral: Idleness brings want.

The Oxen and the Wheels

A pair of oxen were drawing a heavily loaded wagon along a miry country road. They had to use all their strength to pull the wagon, but they did not complain. The wheels of the wagon were of a different sort. Though the task they had to do was very light compared with that of the oxen, they creaked and groaned at every turn. The poor oxen, pulling with all their might to draw the wagon through the deep mud, had their ears filled with the loud complaining of the wheels. And this, you may well know, made their work so much the harder to endure. "Silence!" the oxen cried at last, out of patience. "What have you wheels to complain about so loudly? We are drawing all the weight, not you, and we are keeping still about it besides."

Moral: Those who complain most often suffer least.

The Farmer and His Sons

A certain farmer, lying at the point of death, called his sons around him and gave his fields and vineyards into their charge, telling them that a treasure lay hidden somewhere in them, within a foot from the ground. His sons thought he spoke of money which he had hidden, and after he was buried, they dug most industriously all over the estate but found nothing. The soil being so well loosened, however, meant that the succeeding crops were of unequalled richness and the sons then found out what their father meant in telling them to dig for hidden treasure.

Moral: Hard work has its own reward.

The Blind Man and the Lame Man

A blind man, being stopped in a bad piece of road, met with a lame man and entreated him to guide him through the difficulty he had got into. "How can I do that," replied the lame man, "since I am barely able to drag myself along? But as you appear to be very strong, if you will carry me, we will seek our fortunes together. It will then be my interest to warn you of anything that may obstruct your way; your feet shall be my feet, and my eyes your eyes."

"With all my heart," returned the blind man, "let us render each other our mutual services." So taking his lame companion on his back, they, by means of their union, travelled on with safety and pleasure.

Moral: Wishes and vulnerabilities can lead to cooperation and triumph.

The Horse and the Loaded Donkey

A horse and a donkey were travelling together, the horse prancing along in its fine trappings, the donkey carrying the heavy weight in its packs with difficulty. "I wish I were you," sighed the donkey. "Nothing to do and well fed, and all that fine harness upon you." The next day, however, there was a great battle, and the horse was wounded to death in the final charge of the day. His friend, the donkey, happened to pass by shortly afterward and found him on the point of death. "I was wrong," said the donkey.

Moral: Everybody carries a different kind of burden.

The Lion and the Three Bulls

A lion had been watching three bulls feeding in an open field. He had tried to attack them several times, but they had kept together and helped each other to drive him off. The lion had little hope of eating them, for he was no match for three strong bulls with their sharp horns and hoofs. But he could not keep away from that field, for it is hard to resist watching a good meal, even when there is little chance of getting it. Then one day, the bulls had a quarrel, and when the hungry lion came to look at them and lick his chops as he was accustomed to do, he found them in separate corners of the field, as far away from one another as they could get. It was now an easy matter for the lion to attack them one at a time, and this he proceeded to do with the greatest satisfaction and relish.

Moral: People are strongest when they stick together.

The Fox and the Pheasants

One moonlight evening, as Master Fox was taking his usual stroll in the woods, he saw a number of pheasants perched quite out of his reach on a limb of a tall old tree. The sly fox soon found a bright patch of moonlight where the pheasants could see him clearly; there he raised himself up on his hind legs and began a wild dance. First he whirled 'round and 'round like a top, then he hopped up and down, cutting all sorts of strange capers. The pheasants stared giddily. They hardly dared blink for fear of losing him out of their sight a single instant. The fox made as if to climb a tree; then he fell over and lay still, playing dead; and in the next instant, he was hopping on all fours, his back in the air, and his bushy tail shaking so that it seemed to throw out silver sparks in the moonlight. By this time, the poor birds' heads were in a whirl. And when the fox began his performance all over again, so dazed did they become that they lost their hold on the limb and fell down one by one to the fox.

Moral: Focusing on danger may cause us to fall victim to it.

The Bear and the Beehives

A bear roaming the woods in search of berries happened on a fallen tree in which a swarm of bees had stored their honey. The bear began to nose around the log very carefully to find out if the bees were at home. Just then, one of the swarm came home from the clover field with a load of sweets. Guessing what the bear was after, the bee flew at him, stung him sharply, and disappeared into the hollow log. The bear lost his temper in an instant and sprang upon the log tooth and claw to destroy the nest. But this only brought out the whole swarm. The poor bear had to take to his heels, and he was able to save himself only by diving into a pool of water.

Moral: Flying into a rage can cause a single injury to turn into a thousand.

The Kid and the Wolf

A frisky young kid had been left by the herdsman on the thatched roof of a sheep shelter to keep him out of harm's way. The kid was browsing near the edge of the roof when he spied a wolf and began to jeer at him, making faces and abusing him to his heart's content. "I hear you," said the wolf, "and I haven't the least grudge against you for what you say or do. When you are up there, it is the roof that's talking, not you."

Moral: Sometimes words that sound brave really aren't.

The Great and the Little Fishes

A fisherman was drawing up a net that he had cast into the sea and was now full of all sorts of fish. The little fish escaped through the meshes of the net and got back into the deep, but the great fish were all caught and hauled into the ship.

Moral: Our insignificance can sometimes save us.

The Dog and the Oyster

There was once a dog who was very fond of eggs. He visited the hen house very often and at last got so greedy that he would swallow the eggs whole. One day, the dog wandered down to the seashore. There he spied an oyster. In a twinkling, the oyster was resting in the dog's stomach, shell and all. It pained the dog a good deal, as you can guess. "I've learned that not all round things are eggs," he said, groaning.

Moral: Greed can cause pain.

The Monkey and the Camel

At a great celebration in honor of King Lion, the monkey was asked to dance for the company. His dancing was very clever indeed, and the animals were all highly pleased with his grace and lightness. The praise that was showered on the monkey made the camel envious. He was very sure that he could dance quite as well as the monkey—if not better—so he pushed his way into the crowd that had gathered around the monkey and, rising on his hind legs, began to dance. But the big hulking camel looked very ridiculous as he kicked out his knotty legs and twisted his long clumsy neck. Besides, the animals found it hard to keep their toes from under his heavy hoofs. At last, when one of his huge feet came within an inch of King Lion's nose, the animals were so disgusted that they set upon the camel in a rage and drove him out into the desert. Shortly afterward, refreshments—consisting mostly of camel's hump and ribs—were served to the company.

Moral: It is absurd to compete with everyone you see.

The Trumpeter Taken Prisoner

Upon the defeat of an army in battle, a trumpeter was taken prisoner. The soldiers were about to put him to death, when he cried, "Nay, gentlemen, why should you kill me? This hand of mine is guiltless of a single life."

"Yes," replied the soldiers; "but with that braying instrument of yours, you incite others, and you must share the same fate as they."

Moral: There are many ways to recognize an enemy.

The Boy and the Filberts

A boy was given permission to put his hand into a pitcher to get some filberts. But he took such a great fistful that he could not draw his hand out again. There he stood, unwilling to give up a single filbert and yet unable to get them all out at once. Vexed and disappointed, he began to cry. "My boy," said his mother, "be satisfied with half the nuts you have taken and you will easily get your hand out. Then perhaps you may have some more filberts some other time."

Moral: A little at a time is often the best way.

The One-Eyed Doe

A doe had had the misfortune to lose one of her eyes and could not see anyone approaching her on that side. So to avoid any danger, she always used to feed on a high cliff near the sea with her good eye looking toward the land. By this means, she could see whenever the hunters approached her on land and often escaped. But the hunters found out that she was blind in one eye and, hiring a boat, rowed under the cliff where she used to feed and shot her from the sea. "Ah," she cried with her dying voice, "You cannot escape your fate."

Moral: A person's blind side is always at risk.

The Dog in the Manger

A dog was asleep in a manger filled with hay and was awakened by the cattle, which came in tired and hungry from working in the field. But the dog would not let them get near the manger and snarled and snapped as if it were filled with the best of meat and bones all for himself. The cattle looked at the dog in disgust. "How selfish he is!" said one. "He cannot eat the hay and yet he will not let us who are so hungry for it eat it!" Now the farmer came in. When he saw how the dog was acting, he seized a stick and drove him out of the stable with many a blow for his selfish behavior.

Moral: It's wrong to begrudge others what you cannot enjoy yourself.

The Eagle and the Beetle

A beetle once begged the eagle to spare a hare that had run to her for protection. But the eagle pounced upon her prey, the sweep of her great wings tumbling the beetle a dozen feet away. Furious at the disrespect shown her, the beetle flew to the eagle's nest and rolled out the eggs. Not one did she spare. The eagle's grief and anger knew no bounds, but she did not know who had done the cruel deed. The next year, the eagle built her nest far up on a mountain crag but the beetle found it and again destroyed the eggs. In despair, the eagle now implored great Jupiter to let her place her eggs in his lap. There none would dare harm them. But the beetle buzzed about Jupiter's head and made him rise to drive her away; as he did, the eggs rolled from his lap. So Jupiter commanded that ever after, while the eagle's eggs lie in the nest in the spring, the beetle will sleep in the ground.

Moral: Even the weakest may find means to avenge a wrong.

The Father and His Sons

A certain father had a family of sons who were forever quarreling among themselves. No words he could say did the least good, so he cast about in his mind for some very striking example that should make them see that discord would lead them to misfortune. One day when the quarreling had been much more violent than usual and each of the sons was moping in a surly manner, he asked one of them to bring him a bundle of sticks. Then, handing the bundle to each of his sons in turn, he told them to try to break it. But although each one tried his best, none was able to do so. The father then untied the bundle and gave the sticks to his sons to break one by one. This they did very easily. "My sons," said the father, "do you not see how certain it is that if you agree with each other and help each other, it will be impossible for your enemies to injure you? But if you are divided among yourselves, you will be no stronger than a single stick in that bundle."

Moral: In unity is strength.

The Bee and Jupiter

A bee ascended to Olympus to present Jupiter with some honey fresh from her combs. Jupiter, delighted with the offering of honey, promised to give her whatever she should ask. She therefore asked him, "Give me a stinger so that if any mortal should approach to take my honey, I may kill him." Jupiter was much displeased, for he loved the race of man but could not refuse the request because of his promise. He thus answered the bee: "You shall have your request, but it will be at the peril of your own life. For if you use your stinger, it shall remain in the wound you make and then you will die from the loss of it."

Moral: Spiteful wishes often backfire.

The Bald Man and the Fly

A fly bit the bare head of a bald man who, endeavoring to destroy it, gave himself a heavy slap. Escaping, the fly said mockingly, "You who have wished to revenge the bite of a tiny insect with death: See what you have done to yourself to add insult to injury?"

Moral: A wise person does not seek revenge for small annoyances.

The Doe and the Fawn

A young fawn once said to his mother, "You are larger than a dog, and swifter, and more used to running, and you have your horns as a defense; why, then, mother, do the hounds frighten you so?" She smiled and said, "I know full well, my son, that all you say is true. I have the advantages you mention, but when I hear even the bark of a single dog, I feel ready to faint and fly away as fast as I can."

Moral: No arguments will give courage to the fearful.

The Wolf and the Kid

There was once a little kid whose growing horns made him think he was a grown-up billy goat and able to take care of himself. So one evening when the flock started home from the pasture and his mother called, the kid paid no heed and kept right on nibbling the tender grass. A little later when he lifted his head, the flock was gone. He was all alone. The sun was sinking. Long shadows came creeping over the ground and a chilly little wind came creeping with them, making scary noises in the grass. The kid shivered as he thought of the terrible wolf. Then he started wildly over the field, bleating for his mother. But not halfway, near a clump of trees, there was the wolf! The kid knew there was little hope for him. "Please, Mr. Wolf," he said, trembling, "I know you are going to eat me. But first please pipe me a tune, for I want to dance and be merry as long as I can." The wolf liked the idea of a little music before eating, so he struck up a merry tune and the kid leaped and frisked gaily. Meanwhile, the flock was moving slowly homeward. In the still evening air, the wolf's piping carried far. The shepherd dogs pricked up their ears. They recognized the song as one the wolf sings before a feast, and in a moment, they were racing back to the pasture. The wolf's song ended suddenly, and as he ran with the dogs at his heels, he called himself a fool for turning piper to please a kid, when he should have stuck to his butcher's trade.

Moral: Do not let anything turn you from your purpose.

The Hunter and the Woodman

A hunter, not very bold, was searching for the tracks of a lion. He asked a man who was felling oaks in the forest if he had seen any marks of his footsteps or knew where his lair was. "I will at once show you the lion himself," said the man.

The hunter, turning very pale and chattering with his teeth from fear, replied, "No, thank you. I did not ask that; it is only his track I am in search of, not the lion himself."

Moral: A hero is brave in deeds as well as words.

The Boy and the Nettles

A boy, stung by a nettle, ran home crying to get his mother to blow on the hurt and kiss it. "Son," said the boy's mother when she had comforted him. "The next time you come near a nettle, grasp it firmly and it will be as soft as silk."

Moral: It is often wise to use all your might.

The Vixen and the Lioness

The fox once observed to the lioness that foxes were very much to be envied in the matter of fruitfulness: Almost every year, for instance, she brings into the world a good litter of cubs while some people only have one at a time and not more than twice or thrice in their lives. This sneer was too pointed to be passed over in silence by the lioness, who replied with a good deal of fire, "What you say is true; you have a great many young at a time, and often. But what are they? Foxes. I have but one, but remember that that one is a lion."

Moral: Value is in the worth, not in the number.

The Goatherd and the Goats

One cold stormy day, a goatherd drove his goats for shelter into a cave, where a number of wild goats had also found their way. The shepherd wanted to make the wild goats part of his flock, so he fed them well. But to his own flock, he gave only enough food to keep them alive. When the weather cleared and the shepherd led the goats out to feed, the wild goats scampered off to the hills. "Is that the thanks I get for feeding you and treating you so well?" complained the shepherd.

"Do not expect us to join your flock," replied one of the wild goats. "We know how you would treat us later on if some strangers should come as we did."

Moral: It is unwise to treat old friends badly for the sake of new ones.

The Father and His Two Daughters

A man had two daughters, one married to a gardener and the other to a tilemaker. After a time, he went to the daughter who had married the gardener and inquired how she was and how all things went with her. She said, "All things are prospering with me, and I have only one wish: that there may be a heavy fall of rain in order that the plants may be well watered."

Not long after, he went to the daughter who had married the tilemaker and likewise inquired of her how she fared; she replied, "I want for nothing and have only one wish: that the dry weather may continue and the sun shine hot and bright so that the bricks might be dried."

He said to her, "If your sister wishes for rain and you for dry weather, with which of the two am I to join my wishes?"

Moral: What helps one person may ruin someone else.

Jupiter and the Monkey

There was once a baby show among the animals in the forest. Jupiter provided the prize. Of course, all the proud mammas from far and near brought their babies. But none got there earlier than the mother monkey. Proudly she presented her baby among the other contestants. As you can imagine, there was quite a laugh when the animals saw the ugly flat-nosed, hairless, pop-eyed little creature. "Laugh if you will," said the mother monkey. "Though Jupiter may not give him the prize, I know that he is the prettiest, sweetest, dearest darling in the world."

Moral: Love sees only beauty.

The Two Goats

Two goats frisking happily on the rocky steeps of a mountain valley chanced to meet, one on each side of a deep chasm through which poured a mighty mountain torrent. The trunk of a fallen tree formed the only means of crossing the chasm, and on this, not even two squirrels could have passed each other in safety. The narrow path would have made the bravest tremble. Not so our goats. Their pride would not permit either to stand aside for the other. One set her foot on the log. The other did likewise. In the middle they met, horn to horn. Neither would give way, and so they both fell and were swept away by the roaring torrent below.

Moral: It is better to yield than to come to misfortune through stubbornness.

The Man and the Lion

A man and a lion chanced to travel in company through the forest. They soon began to quarrel, for each of them boasted that he and his kind were far superior to the other both in strength and mind. They reached a clearing in the forest and there stood a statue. It was a representation of Heracles in the act of tearing the jaws of the Nemean Lion. "See," said the man, "That's how strong we are! The King of Beasts is like wax in our hands!"

"Ho!" laughed the lion. "A man made that statue. It would have been quite a different scene had a lion made it!"

Moral: The story all depends on the point of view and who tells it.

The Hare and the Tortoise

A hare was making fun of the tortoise one day for being so slow. "Do you ever get anywhere?" he asked with a mocking laugh.

"Yes," replied the tortoise, "and I get there sooner than you think. I'll run you a race and prove it." The hare was much amused at the idea of running a race with the tortoise, but for the fun of the thing, he agreed. So the fox, who had consented to act as judge, marked the distance and started the runners off. The hare was soon far out of sight and to make the tortoise feel very deeply how ridiculous it was for him to try to race with a hare, lay down beside the course to take a nap until the tortoise should catch up. The tortoise meanwhile kept going slowly but steadily and, after a time, passed the place where the hare was sleeping. But the hare slept on very peacefully; and when at last he did wake up, the tortoise was near the goal. The hare now ran his swiftest, but he could not overtake the tortoise in time.

Moral: Slow and steady wins the race.

Hercules and the Wagoner

A farmer was driving his wagon along a miry country road after a heavy rain. The horses could hardly drag the load through the deep mud, and at last they came to a standstill when one of the wheels sank to the hub in a rut. The farmer climbed down from his seat and stood beside the wagon looking at it but without making the least effort to get it out of the rut. All he did was to curse his bad luck and call loudly on Hercules to come to his aid. Then Hercules really did appear, saying, "Put your shoulder to the wheel, man, and urge on your horses. Do you think you can move the wagon by simply looking at it and whining about it? Hercules will not help unless you make some effort to help yourself." And when the farmer put his shoulder to the wheel and urged on the horses, the wagon moved very readily. Soon the farmer was riding along in great content and with a good lesson learned.

Moral: Self-help is often the best help.

The Wolf and the House Dog

There was once a wolf who got very little to eat because the dogs of the village were so wide awake and watchful. He was really nothing but skin and bones, and it made him very downhearted to think of it. One night, this wolf happened to fall in with a fine fat house dog who had wandered a little too far from home. The wolf would gladly have eaten him then and there, but the house dog looked strong enough to leave his marks should he try it. So the wolf spoke very humbly to the dog, complimenting him on his fine appearance. "You can be as well-fed as I am if you want to," replied the dog. "Leave the woods; there you live miserably. Why, you have to fight hard for every bite you get. Follow my example and you will get along beautifully."

"What must I do?" asked the wolf.

"Hardly anything," answered the house dog. "Chase people who carry canes, bark at beggars, and fawn on the people of the house. In return, you will get tidbits of every kind: chicken bones, choice bits of meat, sugar, cake, and much more beside, not to speak of kind words and caresses."

The wolf had such a beautiful vision of his coming happiness that he almost wept. But just then, he noticed that the hair on the dog's neck was worn and the skin was chafed. "What is that on your neck?"

"Nothing at all," replied the dog.

"What nothing!"

"Oh, just a trifle!"

"But please tell me."

"Perhaps you see the mark of the collar to which my chain is fastened."

"What? A chain!" cried the wolf. "Don't you go wherever you please?"

"Not always. But what's the difference?" replied the dog.

"All the difference in the world! I don't care a rap for your feasts and I wouldn't take all the tender young lambs in the world at that price." And away ran the wolf to the woods.

Moral: There is nothing worth so much as liberty.

The Swallow and the Other Birds

It happened that a countryman was sowing some hemp seeds in a field where a swallow and some other birds were hopping about picking up their food. "Beware of that man," warned the swallow.

"Why, what is he doing?" said the others.

"That is hemp seed he is sowing; be careful to pick up every one of the seeds or else you will repent." The birds paid no heed to the swallow's words, and by and by the hemp grew up and was made into cord, and of the cords nets were made, and many a bird that had despised the swallow's advice was caught in nets made out of that very hemp. "What did I tell you?" said the swallow.

Moral: It's not wise to dismiss advice without considering it.

The Crow and the Pitcher

In a spell of dry weather, when the birds could find very little to drink, a thirsty crow found a pitcher with a little water in it. But the pitcher was high and had a narrow neck and no matter how he tried, the crow could not reach the water. The poor thing felt as if he must die of thirst. Then an idea came to him. Picking up some small pebbles, he dropped them into the pitcher one by one. With each pebble, the water rose a little higher until at last, it was near enough so he could drink.

Moral: In a tight spot, a good use of our wits may help us out.

The Eagle and the Jackdaw

An eagle, swooping down on powerful wings, seized a lamb in her talons and made off with it to her nest. A jackdaw saw the deed, and his silly head was filled with the idea that he was big and strong enough to do as the eagle had done. So with much rustling of feathers and a fierce air, he came down swiftly on the back of a large ram. But when he tried to rise again, he found that he could not get away for his claws were tangled in the wool. And so far was he from carrying away the ram that the ram hardly noticed he was there. The shepherd saw the fluttering jackdaw and at once guessed what had happened. Running up, he caught the bird and clipped its wings. That evening, he gave the jackdaw to his children. "What a funny bird this is!" they said, laughing. "What do you call it, father?"

"That is a jackdaw, my children. But if you should ask him, he would say he is an eagle."

Moral: Vanity can make you overestimate your powers.

The Dancing Monkeys

A prince had some monkeys trained to dance. Being naturally great mimics of men's actions, they showed themselves most apt pupils; and when arrayed in their rich clothes and masks, they danced as well as any of the courtiers. The spectacle was often repeated with great applause, until on one occasion, a courtier, bent on mischief, took from his pocket a handful of peanuts and threw them upon the stage. The monkeys, at the sight of the peanuts, forgot their dancing and became (as indeed they were) monkeys instead of actors and, pulling off their masks and tearing their robes, they fought with one another for the peanuts. The dancing spectacle thus came to an end amidst the laughter and ridicule of the audience.

Moral: Those who pretend will reveal themselves by their actions.

The Hare and the Hound

A dog, having given a long chase to a fine hare that showed himself to be a splendid runner, was at length forced, by want of breath, to give up the pursuit. The owner of the dog thereupon taunted him for having allowed himself to be beaten by the hare. "Ah, master," answered the dog, "it's all very well for you to laugh, but we had different risks. He was running for his life, while I was only running for my dinner."

Moral: Motivation makes all the difference.

The Woodman and the Serpent

One wintry day, a woodman was tramping home from his work when he saw something black lying on the snow. When he came closer, he saw it was a serpent, which was to all appearances dead. But he took it up and put it in his coat to warm while he hurried home. As soon as he got indoors, he put the serpent down on the hearth before the fire. The children watched it and saw it slowly come to life again. One of them stooped down to stroke it, but the serpent raised its head and showed its fangs and was about to bite the child to death. So the woodman seized his axe and, with one stroke, cut the serpent in two. "Ah," he said, "there is no gratitude from the wicked."

Moral: Sometimes help causes great damage.

The Eagle and the Arrow

An eagle was soaring through the air when it suddenly heard the whiz of an arrow and felt itself wounded to death. Slowly it fluttered down to the earth, with its lifeblood pouring out of it. Looking down upon the arrow with which it had been pierced, it found that the shaft of the arrow had been feathered with one of its own plumes. "Alas!" it cried as it died. "Bitter is it to die but doubly bitter to find that I have helped to speed the means of my death!"

Moral: We often give our enemies the means for our own destruction.

The Fox and the Leopard

A fox and a leopard, resting lazily after a generous dinner, amused themselves by disputing about their good looks. The leopard was very proud of his glossy, spotted coat and made disdainful remarks about the fox, whose appearance he declared was quite ordinary. The fox prided himself on his fine bushy tail with its tip of white, but he was wise enough to see that he could not rival the leopard in looks. Still, he kept up a flow of sarcastic talk, just to exercise his wits and to have the fun of arguing. The leopard was about to lose his temper when the fox got up, yawning lazily. "You may have a very smart coat," he said, "but you would be a great deal better off if you had a little more smartness inside your head and less on your ribs, the way I am. That's what I call real beauty."

Moral: A fine coat is not always an indication of a brilliant mind.

The Porcupine and the Snakes

A porcupine was looking for a good home. At last, he found a little sheltered cave where lived a family of snakes. He asked them to let him share the cave with them, and the snakes kindly consented. The snakes soon wished they had not given him permission to stay. His sharp quills pierced them at every turn, and at last, they politely asked him to leave. "I am very well satisfied, thank you," said the porcupine. "I intend to stay right here." And with that, he politely escorted the snakes outside. To save their skins, the snakes had to look for another home.

Moral: An inconsiderate guest can wear out their welcome.

The Crab and Its Mother

"Why in the world do you walk sideways like that?" said a mother crab to her son. "You should always walk straight forward with your toes turned out."

"Show me how to walk, mother dear," answered the little crab obediently. "I want to learn." So the old crab tried and tried to walk straight forward. But she could only walk sideways, like her son. And when she wanted to turn her toes out, she tripped and fell on her nose.

Moral: It's not good to try to persuade someone to act in a way that's uncomfortable to them.

The Lion, the Bear, and the Fox

Just as a great bear rushed to seize a stray lamb, a lion leaped from another direction upon the same prey. The two fought furiously for the prize until they had received so many wounds that both sank down, unable to continue the battle. Just then, a fox dashed up and, seizing the lamb, made off with it as fast as he could go while the lion and the bear looked on in helpless rage. "How much better it would have been," they said, "to have shared in a friendly spirit."

Moral: When fierce competition gets out of control, winners become losers.

The Bull and the Goat

A bull once escaped from a lion by entering a cave that the goatherds used to house their flocks in stormy weather and at night. It happened that one of the goats had been left behind, and the bull had no sooner got inside than this goat lowered his head and made a rush at him, butting him with his horns. As the lion was still prowling outside the entrance to the cave, the bull had to submit to the insult. "Do not think," he said, "that I submit to your cowardly treatment because I am afraid of you. When that lion leaves, I'll teach you a lesson you won't forget."

Moral: It is dangerous to take advantage of another's distress.

Appendix

LESSON PLANS: UNITS AT A GLANCE

by Kayla Briseño

The numbers below correspond with Gretchen Bernabei's books and online resources (please refer to the legend below the chart).

Beginning of Year: Unit Zero—Setting the Stage **(2–3 Weeks)**	**Unit Overview:** *This unit is not tied to a genre but is meant to set the stage for the year. This is a good time to build routines, set expectations (such as regularly sharing our writing and expecting feedback for revision), set up the writer's notebook, do a book tasting to jumpstart reader's workshop, and practice processes that you will continue throughout the year.* • Set up daily journal writing (12) • Set up reader's workshop/book tasting • Generating topics: Create quicklists, heart maps, and idea banks (2, 10) • Write a few kernel essays to set up the writing process: Create a quicklist, write a kernel essay, share with a partner, share with the whole class (1, 2, 3). *Consider using some of the text structures from your upcoming genre/unit.* • Flipbooks (2), "popping" or expanding kernel essays (2) • Introduce *Grammar Keepers* during the third week (start with common errors) (12)
Memoir **(6 Weeks)**	**Unit Overview:** *The memoir unit is ideal to start the year. For many students, writing about themselves is attainable and can lead to confidence in writing in other genres. Students will learn to tell their own story in a way that is interesting for others to read by using details and writer's craft and focusing on (and exploding) a small moment.* **Daily**: Journal writing, "star points" (*Grammar Keepers* lessons), reader's workshop, students sharing their reading and writing, looking for and sharing sparkling sentences from student writing (2, 7) • **Generating Topics:** Narrative quicklist (1, 2, 10) • **Text Structures:** Memory structure (1, 2, 3, 4, 5, 7, 10), story of my thinking (1, 2, 3, 4, 10), memory reflection (1, 2, 3, 4, 10), text structures for stories and other narratives (6)

(Continued)

(Continued)

	• **Mentor Texts:** "I Remember" (8); "My Mother's Tortilla" (8); "Parting" (8); "I Wandered Lonely as Cloud" (8); "Fishing With Grandpa (4 [color it up]); "Tae Kwon Do" (4 [pitchforks]); "New Friend" (4 [dialogue]); "I Do" (4 [exploding a moment]); "Barbie" (4 [naming and renaming])
	• **Author's Craft Mini Lessons:** Ba-da-bing video (11), pitchfork video (11), indelible moments (3), writer's toolbox/adding details (1, 2, 7, 10), icon glossary (3, 7, 10), levels of personal experience (2), exploding the moment (4), naming and renaming (4), color it up (2, 4), 3 icons/3 minutes (3), truisms (2, 7, 10, 11), flipbooks (2), craft challenges (2, 4, 7), lessons found in Part 1 of *Fun-Size Academic Writing for Serious Learning* (4)
	• *Grammar Keepers* **Lessons:** Punctuating beginning/ending of sentence; ba-da-bings (1, 2, 7, 10, 11, 12), pitchforks aka numeration (4, 12), commas in a series, punctuating dialogue, comma in a direct address, common errors
	End Product Options: "I Remember" poems, personal narrative essays, graphic memoirs, published flipbooks, narrative poems, student-narrated videos
Correspondence (3 Weeks)	**Unit Overview:** *This unit can be done at any point in the year and is useful for a breather between more demanding genres. Students will learn the different reasons we write to others by reading and writing next to a variety of mentor texts. These skills can be applied to personal letters, professional letters, fan letters, emails, and even texts and tweets!* **Daily:** Journal writing, "star points" (*Grammar Keepers* lessons), reader's workshop, students sharing their reading and writing, looking for and sharing sparkling sentences from student writing (2, 7) • **Generating Topics:** Heart map (people in my life) (10) • **Text Structures:** Unsent messages (assorted) (10) • **Mentor Texts:** "Letter to William and Mary College" (5), "Letter to Harriet Beecher Stowe" (5), "JFK's Berlin Address" (5), Travis' Letter from the Alamo (5), Humpty Dumpty (6 [apology]) • **Author's Craft Mini Lessons:** Unsent message/heart map (10) • *Grammar Keepers* **Lessons:** Comma in a date, comma between city and state, letter closings **End Product Options:** Email to a teacher; letter to future self; letter to someone—friends, family, authors, heroes, civic leaders, businesses (to actually be mailed)

Research/Info (6 Weeks)	**Unit Overview:** *Research doesn't have to look like it did in the past. Topics of interest and creative final products (beyond a simple research paper or trifold board) are what drive students to dig into this unit and surprise us with their passions.* *Limited on time? This unit would work well in combination with persuasive.* **Daily:** Journal writing, "star points" (*Grammar Keepers* lessons), reader's workshop, students sharing their reading and writing, looking for and sharing sparkling sentences from student writing (2, 7)

- **Generating Topics:** Student topic list (2), quicklists for other genres (2), mining journals for ideas (3)

- **Text Structures:** Informative/expository text structures (2, 3, 4, 10), gritty life (3, 10), basic informational structures (10), structures for explaining a concept (7); infoshots/cubing (3), favorite place (10), problem/solution and defining a concept (4), explanation of a term (3), doing something 101 (3), curiosity (3), teaching someone how to do something (6), sightseeing (5), tour of an unfamiliar place (5), how bullying works (5), the fight (6), three questions (6), what my pet might do (6), the thing I love to do (8), controversial current event (8)

- **Mentor Texts:** Declaration of Independence (problem/solution text structure for research project) (5), lessons found in Part 2 of *Fun-Size Academic Writing for Serious Learning* (4), "Observations on a Steamboat Between Pittsburgh and Cincinnati" (Charles Dickens) (5), "Factory Life" (5), "Journal of a Lady of Quality" (5), "Tweedle Dee and Tweedle Dumb" (6), "Little Tommy Tucker" (6), "Higglety Pigglety" (6), "Because of Libraries We Can Say These Things" (8), "On the Capture and Imprisonment of Crazy Snake, January, 1900" (8)

- **Author's Craft Mini Lessons:** QA12345 (9, 10), infoshots/cubing (3, 7, 10), three-in-one infoshots (3), lessons found in Part 2 of *Fun-Size Academic Writing for Serious Learning* (4), the elastic kernel (3)

- ***Grammar Keepers* Lessons:** Quotations, capitalizing first words in quotations, capitalization, common errors

End Product Options: Research papers, infographics, brochures/pamphlets, commercials, presentations, current event reports, web pages, Instagram accounts, zines, poetry collections (such as *Radium Girls*) showcasing research

(Continued)

(Continued)

Persuasive/ Argument/ Opinion (6 Weeks)	**Unit Overview:** *It can be said that just about any genre is a form of argument, which makes this unit so important and versatile. Students will learn real-world situations where persuasive skills are necessary, both orally and in writing.*
	Daily: Journal writing, "star points" (*Grammar Keepers* lessons), reader's workshop, students sharing their reading and writing, looking for and sharing sparkling sentences from student writing (2, 7)
	• **Generating topics:** Gritty life quicklist (3, 10), mining journals for ideas (3)
	• **Text Structures:** 11-minute essay (3, 4, 7, 8), "Picking Up the Pieces" (5), problem–solution message (5), structures for unfairness (6), text structures for problem solving (6), defining a concept (4), time for a real solution (5), "Breaking Into a Heated Argument" (5), S.O.S. (5), "A Bad Situation A Lot of Us Are In" (5), text structures useful as persuasion about needed change (5), ethos (3), pathos (3), logos (3)
	• **Mentor Texts:** "Pearl Harbor Address to the Nation" (5), "Kimberlie Gonzalez, 7th Grade 11-Minute Essay" (7), "Letter to a Cockroach, Now Dead and Mixed Into a Bar of Chocolate" (8), "Declaration of Independence" (5), "Victory or Death: Letter from the Alamo William B Travis" (5), "Ain't I a Woman?: Speech, Sojourner Truth" (5), "Common Sense" (5), "I'd Rather Not Be on Relief" (5), any of the fairytales and corresponding truisms from *Text Structures from Fairy Tales* (7)
	• **Author's Craft Mini Lessons:** Truisms (2, 7, 10, 11), QA12345 (9, 10), 11-minute essay (use this strategy with *any* text structure—3, 4, 7, 8), dead giveaways (7, 10), jerk talk (13), truism braid (7, 10, 11), build an opinion prompt (3), lessons found in Part 3 of *Fun-Size Academic Writing for Serious Learning* (4), the elastic kernel (3), rhetorical moves/devices (4)
	• *Grammar Keepers* **Lessons:** Sentence wringer, paragraph overhaul, AAAWWUBBIS, apostrophes, commas in beginning/ending phrases
	End Product Options: Advertisements, debates, letters to the editor, proposals, book/movie/restaurant/video game/theme park (anything really!) reviews, argumentative essays, 11-minute essays, Op-Eds, multigenre character moments of persuasion (9 [appendix], 13 [Lesson 21]), literary thematic essays, visual truism collages centered around a theme, short answer responses
Fiction (4 Weeks)	**Unit Overview:** *Thomas Newkirk (2005) says our brains are wired for story. During this often-anticipated unit (a perfect one for the doldrums of right before or after spring break), students will write craft-filled stories by reading tons of mentor texts (such as picture books!) and applying many of the strategies learned in the memoir unit.*

Daily: Journal writing, "star points" (*Grammar Keepers* lessons), reader's workshop, students sharing their reading and writing, looking for and sharing sparkling sentences from student writing (2, 7)

- **Generating Topics:** Narrative quicklist (for a character), heart map (for a character) (10), mining journals for ideas (3)

- **Text Structures:** A fable (1, 3, 9), a sequel to a fable (1, 3, 9), a completely made-up story (1, 9), text structures for stories and other narratives (6)

- **Mentor Texts**: Fables (9), fairy tales (7), various pieces found in Part 1 of *Fun-Size Academic Writing for Serious Learning* (4)

- **Author's Craft Mini Lessons:** Writer's toolbox/adding details (1, 2, 7, 10), icon glossary (3, 7, 10), point of view (4), flashbacks (4), flash-forwards (4), foreshadowing (4), exploding the moment (4), layering thinking with dialogue (4), the list of "25 More Things to Do With These Lessons" in Appendix #2 of *Text Structures From Fairy Tales* (7), lessons found in Part 1 of *Fun-Size Academic Writing for Serious Learning* (4)

- *Grammar Keepers* **Lessons**: Common errors, spelling, chicken dance (punctuating dialogue)

End Product Options: Short stories, graphic novels, picture books (that they can then share with a younger class), zines, web comics, fan fiction, imagined dialogue between famous people, sequels to favorite stories, fictionalized historical moments, stop-motion animated videos, plays, multiple-voice stories, stories using multiple flashbacks, poems as stories, dialogue as stories, journal entries as stories, ekphrastic stories (such as *The Mysteries of Harris Burdick* by Chris Van Allsburg [1984]), multigenre projects, epistolary stories

Poetry (3+ Weeks)	**Unit Overview:** *Whether you routinely share poems or you save poetry for its own unit, poems are a quick way to teach a variety of skills and devices. Not only will poems be a catalyst for rich discussions, they can also be used to inspire original poems and are useful tools to practice reading response techniques. This would be an ideal unit to spiral throughout the year by introducing a weekly poem.*
	
	Daily: Journal writing, "star points" (*Grammar Keepers* lessons), reader's workshop, students sharing their reading and writing, looking for and sharing sparkling sentences from student writing (2, 7)
	
	    • **Generating Topics:** Mining journals for ideas (3)
	
	    • **Mentor Texts:** Selections from the *Text Structures From Poetry* book (8)

(Continued)

(Continued)

	• **Author's Craft Mini Lessons:** Mining journals (3), review icon glossary (3, 7, 10), glossary of poetic terms (10), "Positive Points for Potential Poets" found in Appendix 5 of *Text Structures From Poetry* (8), "How Can I Improve My Poem?" found in Appendix 6 of *Text Structures From Poetry* (8), various lessons in the Appendix of *Text Structures from Poetry* (8) • *Grammar Keepers* **Lessons**: Parts of speech, beyond verbs, pitchforking **End Product Options:** Student-written poems, chapbooks, poetry collections (centered around a topic or theme or trying out different types of poetry), illustrated poems, poetry cafe/open mic/poetry slam, spoken-word poems, poetry videos, ekphrastic poems, and imitation poems (borrowing the style, spacing, language, craft, or structure from an original poem), song lyrics

Response to Reading
(All Year Long)
	Unit Overview: *Response to reading really happens all year long. When we are reading whole-class novels; when students are engaged in book clubs; when mentor texts are shared; whenever texts such as picture books, poems, short stories, and articles are read and discussed; or occasionally when students are reading their choice of novels for reader's workshop, there is the opportunity to respond to reading. The strategies in this collection are meant to be woven throughout the whole year.*
	
	Daily: Journal writing, "star points" (*Grammar Keepers* lessons), reader's workshop, students sharing their reading and writing, looking for and sharing sparkling sentences from student writing (2, 7)
	
	• **Generating Topics:** Student independent reading, teacher-choice mentor texts, whole class novels, and book club novels
	
	• **Text Structures:**
	
	   o **Text Structures for Basic Reader's Response:** Story of my thinking, character feelings, making a connection, summary, the effect of an author's choice (all from 9, 10)
	
	   o **Text Structures for Great Lines**: I knew that!, how I figured it out/cracking the code, did I miss something, the path of wondering, clarifier—aha (all from 9, 10)
	
	   o **Q&A—About Understanding the Reading**: QA12345, RACE, ba-da-binging the evidence, figuring out the reading, explaining a change (all from 9, 10)
	
	   o **Five Handy Ways to Respond to Reading**: QA12345, infoshots/cubing, ba-da-bings, three-things response, one-liners (all from 9, 10)

- ○ **Q &A—Author's Choice:** RACE, noticing the author's moves, the effect on the reader, the effect of an author's choice (all from 9, 10)

- **Author's Craft Mini Lessons:** Kernelizing a mentor text, an article, a poem, a speech, a letter, a song, or a reading passage and extracting the structure for student writing (3, 5, 6, 7, 8, 9); write a question and pick a structure (9); one-line exploration (9); Strand 5 "green heads" aka author's tools and effect on reader (9); book report essays (3, 7); lullaby weave (1)

End Product Options: Exit tickets, kernel essays using the text structures for response (9); short-answer questions, open-ended responses, multigenre character moments of persuasion (9 [Appendix], 13 [Lesson 21]); multimedia analysis of a literary theme (4 [Lesson 67]); one-liners (9); three-things responses (9); ba-da-bings (9)

Legend: 1. *Reviving the Essay*

2. *Crunchtime*

3. *The Story of My Thinking*

4. *Fun-Size Academic Writing for Serious Learning*

5. *Text Structures From the Masters*

6. *Text Structures From Nursery Rhymes*

7. *Text Structures From Fairy Tales*

8. *Text Structures From Poetry*

9. *Text Structures From Fables*

10. www.trailofbreadcrumbs.net

11. Trail of Breadcrumbs YouTube Channel

12. *Grammar Keepers*

13. *Why We Must Run With Scissors*

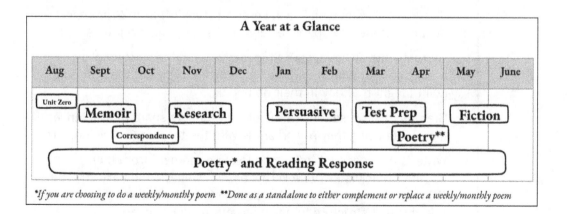

LESSON PLANS: A WEEK AT A GLANCE (AND THEN SOME)

*Lessons based on a 45-minute period in a secondary classroom

Week 1	Lessons from a Memoir Unit
Notes	• In a 45-minute period, the reader's workshop block may need to be shortened or included on alternating days.
	• Reader's workshop can include such things as independent reading, small group or independent conferencing, and the occasional reading response, but it is important to let students read self-selected books as often as possible.
	• **While it may be tempting to skip things such as the grammar conversation or the sharing of student writing for time's sake, don't do it! This is where the real work and learning happens, so it is a must. Those conversations need to be external before they become internal.**
	• **Regularly having students share their writing (with partners as well as with the whole class) is a mainstay of any successful literacy classroom. Allowing space for this almost daily is necessary.**
	• It's important to read and write with your students. If they are reading, try your best to read with them (keeping one teacher eye out, of course!). If they are writing, write along with them and share what you've done! Share your struggles and the things you did to get past the hard part. Having your students see you model what being a reader and writer should look like is so powerful and goes a long way!
	• The lessons in *Grammar Keepers* are meant to be done in response to the needs of students, so while these lesson plans follow the order in which *Grammar Keepers* is written, you should follow the order that your students need.
Day 1	• Reader's Workshop (15 minutes), Book Talks (2 minutes): Students read their books of choice independently and then share book recommendations with a partner and/or with the class.
	• Star Point (2 minutes): Teach Lesson 1 (*they're*) from *Grammar Keepers*; students copy notes and try the argument on the script.
	• Journal Time (10 minutes): Students write in their notebooks on a topic of their choice and are encouraged to try out the grammar point taught that day in their notebook.
	• Grammar Conversations (2 minutes): Students share the sentences they wrote using *they're* and argue with the teacher (2–3 volunteers).
	• Writer's Workshop (15 minutes): Using a moment from their narrative quicklist, write a kernel essay using the memory structure (10 minutes), and share with a partner/the whole class (5 minutes). Add this text structure to a text structure anchor chart.
	○ Homework: Read for 20 minutes.

Week 1	Lessons From a Memoir Unit
Day 2	• Reader's Workshop (15 minutes), Book Talks (2 minutes): Students read their books of choice independently and then share book recommendations with a partner and/or with the class. • Star Point (2 minutes): Teach Lesson 2 (*there*) from *Grammar Keepers*; students copy notes and try the argument on the script. • Journal Time (10 minutes): Students write in their notebooks on a topic of their choice and are encouraged to try out the grammar point taught that day in their notebook. • Grammar Conversations (2 minutes): Students share the sentences they wrote using *there* and argue with the teacher (2–3 volunteers). • Writer's Workshop (15 minutes): Using their narrative quicklist and the same memory structure, students will write another kernel essay about a different moment and share with a partner/the whole class. o Homework: Read for 20 minutes and share one of their kernel essays with at least two people outside of class. (Get their signatures!)
Day 3	• Reader's Workshop (15 minutes), Book Talks (2 minutes): Students read their books of choice independently and then share book recommendations with a partner and/or with the class. • Star Point (2 minutes): Teach Lesson 3 (*their*) from *Grammar Keepers;* students copy notes and try the argument on the script. • Journal Time (10 minutes): Students write in their notebooks on a topic of their choice and are encouraged to try out the grammar point taught that day in their notebook. • Grammar Conversations (2 minutes): Students share the sentences they wrote using *their* and argue with the teacher (2–3 volunteers). • Writer's Workshop (15 minutes): Using their narrative quicklist and the same memory structure, students will write another kernel essay about a different moment and share with a partner/the whole class. o Homework: Read for 20 minutes and share their favorite of the three kernel essays with at least three people outside of class. (Get their signatures!)
Day 4	• Reader's Workshop (15 minutes), Book Talks (2 minutes): Students read their books of choice independently and then share book recommendations with a partner and/or with the class. • Star Point (2 minutes): Teach Lesson 4 (*too*) from *Grammar Keepers*; students copy notes and try the argument on the script. • Journal Time (10 minutes): Students write in their notebooks on a topic of their choice and are encouraged to try out the grammar point taught that day in their notebook. • Grammar Conversations (2 minutes): Students share the sentences they wrote using *too* and argue with the teacher (2–3 volunteers).

(Continued)

(Continued)

Week 1	Lessons From a Memoir Unit
Day 4	• Writer's Workshop (15 minutes): Teach the mini lesson "levels of personal experience" (2 minutes). Then have students gather in small groups or partnerships and share their kernel essays with the goal of picking the best one to "pop" or expand (preferably a Level 2 or 3). If students have not written a Level 2 or 3 story, they should try writing one in class or for homework. ○ Homework: Read for 20 minutes and write a memory structure kernel essay about one of the characters from the book they are reading.
Day 5	• Reader's Workshop (15 minutes), Book Talks (2 minutes): Students read their books of choice independently and then share book recommendations with a partner and/or with the class. • Star Point (2 minutes): Teach Lesson 5 (*two*) from *Grammar Keepers*; students copy notes and try the argument on the script. • Journal Time (10 minutes): Students write in their notebooks on a topic of their choice and are encouraged to try out the grammar point taught that day in their notebook. • Grammar Conversations (2 minutes): Students share the sentences they wrote using *two* and argue with the teacher (2–3 volunteers). • Writer's Workshop (15 minutes): Students should have a kernel essay read to "pop" (expand/add details). Allow them time to add details and tell the rest of the story by turning each sentence into at least one paragraph. They may need to add more paragraphs of "what happened next" and that is great! Optional: Teach students how to use the flipbook or a fake flipbook. ○ Homework: Read for 20 minutes. Optional: Finish drafting their "popped" kernel essay (if class time will not permit more drafting time).
Day 6	• Reader's Workshop (15 minutes), Book Talks (2 minutes): Students read their books of choice independently and then share book recommendations with a partner and/or with the class. • Star Point (2 minutes): Teach Lesson 6 (*to*) from *Grammar Keepers*; students copy notes and try the argument on the script. • Journal Time (10 minutes): Students write in their notebooks on a topic of their choice and are encouraged to try out the grammar point taught that day in their notebook. • Grammar Conversations (2 minutes): Students share the sentences they wrote using *to* and argue with the teacher (2–3 volunteers). • Writer's Workshop (15 minutes): If time allows, have students continue drafting their essays as you conference with small groups to determine needs for future mini lessons.

Week 1	Lessons From a Memoir Unit
	• Mini Lesson: Teach ba-da-bings (1, 2, 10, 11, 12) and have students try them in their own memoirs. Add the three icons (action, seeing, and thinking) to the writer's toolbox (or writer's craft) anchor chart. • Homework: Read for 20 minutes. Add at least two ba-da-bings to drafts. Optional: Students who are not finished with their drafts should complete them by the next class.
Day 7	• Reader's Workshop (15 minutes), Book Talks (2 minutes): Students read their books of choice independently and then share book recommendations with a partner and/or with the class. • Star Point (2 minutes): Teach Lesson 7 (*it's*) from *Grammar Keepers*; students copy notes and try the argument on the script. • Journal Time (10 minutes): Students write in their notebooks on a topic of their choice and are encouraged to try out the grammar point taught that day in their notebook. • Grammar Conversations (2 minutes): Students share the sentences they wrote using *it's* and argue with the teacher (2–3 volunteers). • Writer's Workshop (15 minutes) • Homework: Read for 20 minutes.

Day 8–end	• Through the unit (and the year!), broaden, deepen, and build the students' learning through reading and writing by doing the following:
	
	   o using additional text structures (one at a time) and adding them to the anchor chart
	
	   o collecting and using writer's craft and adding their icons (with examples) to the writer's toolbox
	
	   o writing and sharing kernel essays
	
	   o discovering and introducing mentor texts to model quality writing in both structure and craft
	
	   o developing ways to respond in writing to what students are reading
	
	   o taking note of any impact that the writer's choices have on their reader

BASIC INFORMATIONAL STRUCTURES

Description

What it is	**Kinds** of it	**Where** you can find it	**Parts** of it	One thing **almost all of them** do

---

Sequence

This is about the **process** of ___.	**Prior to** ___, this happens.	**After** ___, this happens.	**When it's time** for ___, this happens.	**Finally,** ___.

Cause and Effect

What happens:	This happens because ___.	That makes ___ happen.	This happens for several reasons, including ___.	As a result, _____.

Compare and Contrast

___ and ___ are very much **alike**.	They **both** ___ **and** ___.	**However**, there are some **differences** between the two.	**For one thing,** ___.	**Another way they are different is** ___.

Problem and Solution

___ is happening.	This is a **problem** because _____.	This is happening **because** _____.	Another thing **contributing to the problem** is _____.	We must stop this **so that** _____.

Question: Do you have any tips on answering open-ended questions?

Answer: I do. In a nutshell, here's the sequence of what I do:

Teaching Students How to Answer a Question (Not in Writing, But Out Loud)

Have the students practice answering questions about themselves, *not* about stories or written text, using the dialogue Q&A format. Do these out loud. Have fun with them. I do two a day (just you and a volunteer at the front of the class in front of everyone, you using the QA12345 script and the other person answering the questions) at the beginning of class and don't tell students that it's even related to testing.

Teaching Them to Answer a Question About a Story They Already Know (Prepare It in Writing So They Can Perform the Dialogue Out Loud)

Have students write questions about movies they've all seen using the generic question stems.

Have them write QA12345 scripts to answer their questions using the dialogue format and then act out their questions and dialogues.

Teaching Them How to Answer a Question From a Story They Just Read (Prepare It in Writing So They Can Perform the Dialogue Out Loud)

Have them write questions about stories they read using the same generic question stems.

Have them write answers to these questions, and on #1 and #3, use *only* quotations of text from the stories.

That's what I do. We don't even try to make them insightful or global, just shoot for an answer with evidence. The above will get passing scores if they do that with the questions from the test. In fact, for questions involving only one text, they can use QA12345 and do well. I advise all of my students to do this, *not* to write tiny little essays. Go for a 2 and move on, saving all that energy for something else, like their composition or lunch.

Teaching Them How to Craft Their Answer Better

Do sentence-combining exercises. Prepare for this by getting one of your own students' released answers from any recent tests and breaking it down into sentence-combining exercises.

Hand them out and ask students to combine the sentences into stronger writing.

Compare answers.

Look at the student's original answer together.

Repeat this process with another high-scoring response, readied for a sentence-combining exercise.

MOMENTS OF PERSUASION IN
THE ODYSSEY

The poet tries to persuade the Muses to help make his story good.

Odysseus tries to persuade everyone that the gods are unnecessary.

The Greeks persuade the Trojans that the war is over.

Odysseus tries to convince his men not to eat the Lotus plant.

Odysseus tries to convince his men to bypass Thrinacia.

Eurylochus tries to persuade Odysseus to sail away from Circe's island.

Odysseus convinces Polyphemus to eat him last.

Polyphemus convinces his dad, Poseidon, to bring wrath on Odysseus.

Athena tries to convince Odysseus not to go straight home.

Penelope tries to persuade the suitors that Odysseus is alive.

The suitors try to get Penelope to decide on one of them.

King Alcinous persuades Odysseus to tell him the whole story.

Hermes convinces Odysseus to take steps to resist Circe's magic.

Odysseus convinces the cyclops to drink more wine.

Aeolus convinces Odysseus not to open the bag of wind until it's time.

Odysseus's crew beg Odysseus to drive the cyclopes' kids and lambs aboard the ship.

Odysseus begs Circe to let his men go home.

One of Odysseus's crew tries to convince Odysseus not to explore Circe's island.

Athena urges Odysseus to visit his faithful swineherd.

Athena tries to convince Telemachus to return home.

Athena urges Telemachus to see the swineherd for a night on his way home.

Odysseus tries to persuade Polyphemus to go get supplies.

Odysseus tries to convince his crew not to eat the sun god's cattle.

Penelope tries to get the suitors out of her house.

Odysseus convinces Circe that he is dangerous.

The suitors persuade Telemachus to leave home (and go look for his father).

Circe tries to convince Odysseus to succumb to her enchanted potion.

Odysseus tries to persuade the gods to hear him.

King Alcinous persuades Odysseus to reveal his identity.

Odysseus persuades the cyclops that his name is "Nohbody."

Polyphemus tries to convince his neighbors that he has been attacked by a mortal.

Odysseus's crew try to persuade him to stop yelling at Polyphemus.

Odysseus urges his men to keep rowing, even though they're being eaten by Scylla.

Odysseus directs the crew to sail toward the Sirens.

Circe convinces Odysseus to stay with her.

Calypso persuades Odysseus to stay with her on the island.

Calypso tries to convince Odysseus to stay with her forever.

Odysseus persuades Calypso that he needs to go home.

Odysseus persuades his men to wait in the cave for the shepherd to return.

Odysseus persuades the cyclops to get drunk.

Odysseus persuades his men to help him burn the eye of the cyclops.

Odysseus persuades Telemachus to wait for revenge until the time is right.

Penelope persuades the suitors to wait for her decision until she finishes weaving.

Penelope persuades the suitors to have a contest to see who gets to marry her.

Polyphemus tries to convince Odysseus that he is stronger than the gods.

Odysseus convinces Penelope that he's an old, old suitor.

Odysseus convinces the lords to hear him.

The suitors try to persuade Penelope that her husband is dead.

The suitors try to persuade Telemachus that his father is dead.

Odysseus persuades his men to row their boat toward Scylla.

Odysseus convinces Calypso to help him build a raft.

Zeus persuades Calypso to let Odysseus go.

Circe tries to convince Odysseus's men to come in and eat.

Eumaeus convinces Odysseus that he is loyal.

Circe convinces Odysseus about all the things he will have to do to get past the Sirens.

Odysseus persuades his crew to put wax in their ears.

Circe convinces Odysseus that his men will all die.

Odysseus persuades his men that they will survive.

The Sirens try to convince Odysseus to come closer.

Odysseus convinces his men to go on to the next challenge, even though some of them have already died.

Argos tries to convince himself that his master will return.

Odysseus convinces his crew to tie him to the mast.

Odysseus tries to tell his crew to untie him from the mast.

Odysseus convinces Telemachus that he is Odysseus.

Odysseus convinces the swineherd and cowherd, his two old faithful friends, that he is truly Odysseus.

Odysseus persuades servants to let the women know they should stay in their rooms, no matter what.

Polyphemus tries to persuade Odysseus to come back.

Penelope persuades the suitors to let Odysseus shoot the bow.

Penelope tries to get the suitors out of her house.

Circe persuades Odysseus that her advice will help him get home.

Odysseus tells Telemachus not to tell anyone that he's back.

Odysseus persuades Eumaeus and the cowherd to lock all the doors.

Odysseus tries to convince Apollo to help him make the shot (with his bow and arrow).

Eurymachus tries to convince Odysseus that Antinous was the ringleader.

Eurymachus tries to convince Odysseus that Antinous led them to pillage the house.

Eurymachus tries to get all the others to rush Odysseus and kill him.

Eurymachus tries to bribe Odysseus not to kill him by offering riches.

Telemachus convinces his father to let him go and get armor for them to fight with.

Athena persuades Odysseus to fight more.

Odysseus makes everyone believe he's an old man.

ENGLISH I. MULTIGENRE PROJECT ON *THE ODYSSEY*

Directions: Choose 10 moments of persuasion and 10 different forms of writing from the genre list. For each, write what the character might have said using your own creative use of form, vocabulary, syntax, style, rhetoric, and color. You should house the collection in an appropriate way, either mounting them into a book, onto a poster, in a hatbox or treasure box, or any other device you imagine.

OVERSIMPLIFIED TEKS SHORT ANSWER RUBRIC

Jack and Jill went up the hill

to fetch a pail of water

Jack fell down and broke his crown

and Jill came tumbling after.

How did Jack change during this nursery rhyme?

Score	Description of response	Example	Comment
0	Didn't address the question	Jack wanted to get some water in a pail.	Huh?
1	Partly answered the question (answer or evidence but not both)	Jack got hurt.	Answer without evidence.
		"Broke his crown."	Evidence without answer.
2	Answered the question with evidence (answer and evidence)	Jack "broke his crown." This means his head was injured.	Answer with evidence.
3	Answered with beauty, insight, or writing craft	Prior to the water-fetching incident, Jack is healthy, whole, and pursuing not only life-sustaining water for his family but also potentially a life-sustaining bond with Jill; after the incident when he "broke his crown," Jack's only choice is to put his goals to the side and convalesce. So the ill-fated water-haul catastrophe not only injures him physically, it derails his life.	Woof.

Question: _____ Answer: _____

1. How do you know?

2. What does that mean?

3. How else do you know?

4. What does that mean?

5. So, your answer is . . . what?

QUESTIONS FOR PRACTICE

What is your name?

What color are your eyes?

Is it hot outside?

How did you get here today?

Is it raining right now?

What is your mom's name?

Which state do you live in?

Where were you born?

What shoes are you wearing?

What color is your hair?

What color is the sky?

What is your favorite color?

When is your birthday?

How many stars are on the United States flag?

What is your favorite dessert?

How many fingers are on your left hand?

What's one thing you can buy at McDonald's?

What color are your fingernails?

Have you seen *The Wizard of Oz*?

What's the name of our school?

Where did you go to middle school?

What's your best grade? (What subject?)

TEN WAYS TO USE BA-DA-BINGS

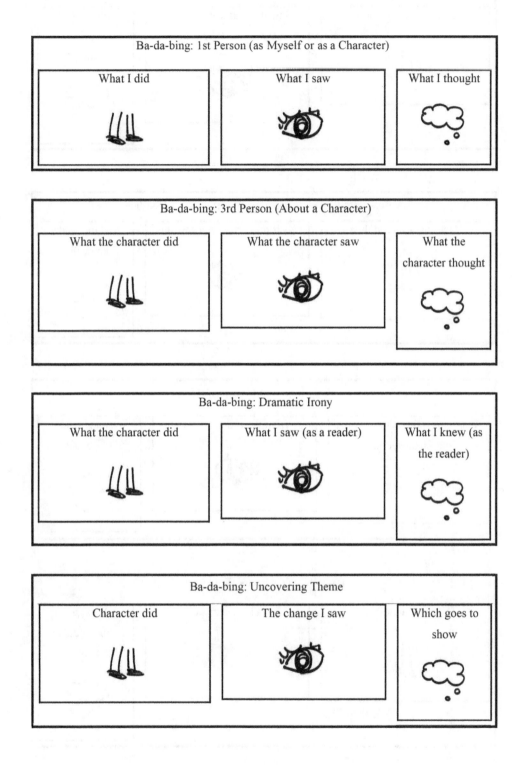

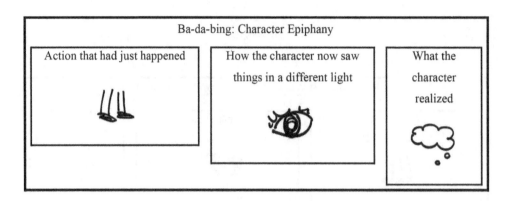

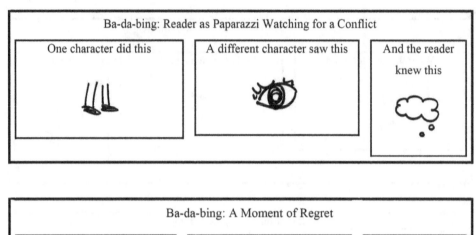

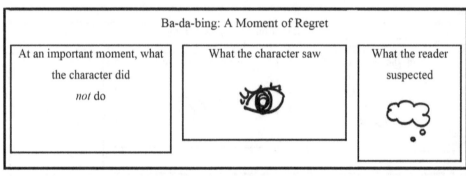

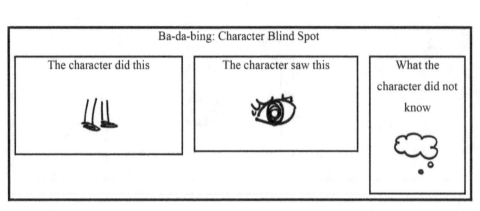

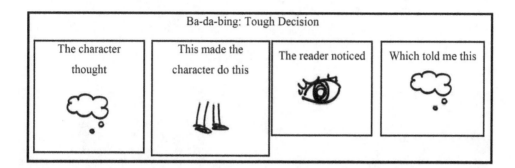

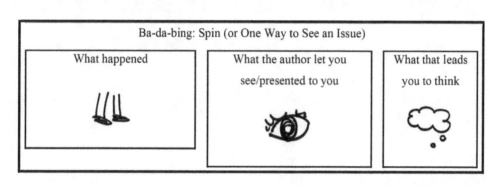

References

Ahearn, J. R., (2010). *Don't call me pruneface!* Scholastic.

Bernabei, G. (2005). *Reviving the essay: How to teach structure without formula.* Discover Writing Company.

Bernabei, G. (2009). *Crunchtime.* Heinemann.

Bernabei, G. (2015). *Grammar keepers: Lessons that tackle students' most persistent problems once and for all, Grades 4–12.* Corwin.

Bernabei, G. (2022). *Trail of Breadcrumbs* [website]. https://trailofbreadcrumbs.net/

Bernabei, G. (2022). *Trail of Breadcrumbs* [YouTube Channel]. YouTube. https://www.youtube.com/c/trailofbreadcrumbs

Bernabei, G., & Hall, D. (2012). *The story of my thinking.* Heinemann.

Bernabei, G., & Koppe, J. (2016). *Text structures from the masters: 50 lessons and nonfiction mentor texts to help students write their way in and read their way out of every single imaginable genre, Grades 6–10.* Corwin.

Bernabei, G., & Reimer, J. (2013). *Fun-size academic writing for serious learning.* Corwin.

Bernabei, G., & Reimer, J. (2019). *Text structures from fairy tales: Truisms that help students write about abstract concepts . . . and live happily ever after, Grades 4–12.* Corwin.

Bernabei, G., Shook, K., & Hover, J. (2017). *Text structures from nursery rhymes: Teaching reading and writing to young children.* Corwin.

Bernabei, G., & Van Prooyen, L. (2020). *Text structures from poetry, Grades 4–12: Lessons to help students read, analyze, and create poems they will remember.* Corwin.

Bernabei, M. (2020). Or forever hold your peace [Song].

Black, S. (2017, February 7). Possums. *Poem-a-day.* Academy of American Poets.

Cowan, E. (1980). *Writing.* Wiley.

Creech, S. (2001). *Love that dog.* HarperCollins.

DiPucchio, K. (2008). *Grace for president.* Little, Brown Books for Young Readers.

Lane, B., & Bernabei, G. (2001). *Why we must run with scissors: Voice lesson in persuasive writing.* Discover Writing Press.

London, J. (1903). *The call of the wild.* Macmillan.

Miller, A. (1953). *The crucible.* Penguin Classics.

Newkirk, T. (2005). *The school essay manifesto: Reclaiming the essay for students and teachers.* Discover Writing Press.

Newkirk, T. (2021). *Writing unbound: How fiction transforms student writers.* Heinemann.

Noden, H. (2011). *Image grammar.* Heinemann.

Palacio, R. J. (2012). *Wonder.* Alfred A. Knopf.

Pinker, S. (2014). *A sense of style.* Penguin.

Shakespeare, W. (1992). *Hamlet.* Simon & Schuster.

Smolan, S. (Director). (1991, April 15). The big kiss (Season 2, Episode 2) [television episode]. In J. Brand & J. Falsey (Creators), *Northern exposure.* Cine-Nevada Productions.

Trivizas, E. (1993). *The three little wolves and the big bad pig.* Heinemann Young Books.

Van Allsburg, C. (1984). *The mysteries of Harris Burdick.* Houghton Mifflin.

Because...

ALL TEACHERS ARE LEADERS

DOMINIQUE SMITH, DOUGLAS FISHER, NANCY FREY

Take an active approach toward disrupting the negative effects of labels and assumptions that interfere with student learning.

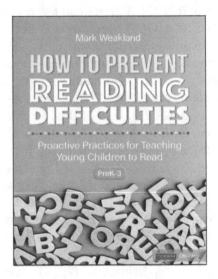

MARK WEAKLAND

Build on decades of evidence and years of experience to understand how the brain learns to read and how to apply that understanding to Tier 1 instruction.

MELANIE MEEHAN, KELSEY SORUM

Learn how to adapt curriculum to meet the needs of the whole child. Each chapter offers intentional steps for responsive instruction across four domains: academic, linguistic, cultural, and social-emotional.

DEBBIE DILLER

Discover concrete guidance for tailoring the small-group experience to literacy instruction in order to give every reader a pathway to success.

To order your copies, visit corwin.com/literacy

At Corwin Literacy we have put together a collection of just-in-time, classroom-tested, practical resources from trusted experts that allow you to quickly find the information you need when you need it.

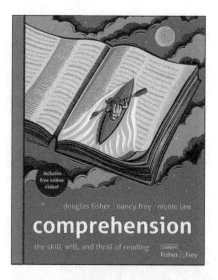

DOUGLAS FISHER, NANCY FREY, NICOLE LAW

Using a structured, three-pronged approach—skill, will, and thrill—students experience reading as a purposeful act with this new comprehensive model of reading instruction.

PAM KOUTRAKOS

Packed with ready-to-go lessons and tools, this user-friendly resource provides ways to weave together different aspects of literacy using one mentor text.

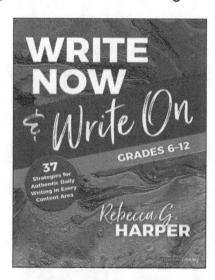

REBECCA G. HARPER

Customizable strategies turn students' informal writing into a springboard for daily writing practice in every content area—with a focus on academic vocabulary, summarizing, and using textual evidence.

MELANIE MEEHAN, CHRISTINA NOSEK, MATTHEW JOHNSON, DAVE STUART JR., MATTHEW R. KAY

This series offers actionable answers to your most pressing questions about teaching reading, writing, and ELA.

A SAGE Publishing Company

Helping educators make the greatest impact

CORWIN HAS ONE MISSION: to enhance education through intentional professional learning.

We build long-term relationships with our authors, educators, clients, and associations who partner with us to develop and continuously improve the best evidence-based practices that establish and support lifelong learning.